A ROOM OF HER OWN

A ROOM OF HER OWN

Women's Personal Spaces

Chris Casson Madden

Photographs by Jennifer Lévy
Design by Dania Martinez Davey

CLARKSON POTTER/PUBLISHERS • NEW YORK

*To three strong and vibrant
women, role models all:
Ann Morrow Lindbergh,
Virginia Woolf, Oprah Winfrey,
and to the phenomenal
women who opened up the doors
to their private
places and whose stories unfold
on the pages that follow.*

*This book is also dedicated
to my mother, Ann, and
my mother-in-law, Mary,
and to my sister, Patty,
who was the reason
for my own personal space.*

COPYRIGHT © 1997 BY CHRIS MADDEN, INC.

PHOTO CREDITS APPEAR ON PAGE 224.

PUBLISHED BY CLARKSON N. POTTER, INC.,
201 EAST 50TH STREET, NEW YORK, NEW YORK 10022.
MEMBER OF THE CROWN PUBLISHING GROUP.

RANDOM HOUSE, INC. NEW YORK,
TORONTO, LONDON, SYDNEY, AUCKLAND
http://www.randomhouse.com/

CLARKSON N. POTTER, POTTER, AND COLOPHON
ARE TRADEMARKS OF CLARKSON N. POTTER, INC.

PRINTED IN CHINA

LIBRARY OF CONGRESS CATALOGING-
IN-PUBLICATION DATA
IS AVAILABLE UPON REQUEST.

ISBN 0-517-59939-2

10 9 8 7 6 5 4 3 2 1

FIRST EDITION

As always, the loving patience of the men in my life—Kevin, Patrick, Nicky, and my dad, Ed—helped make this book a reality.

I am grateful to my brilliant editor, Annetta Hanna, who planted the seed of this idea in my brain. Without her there would be no book. Her gentle guidance and insightfulness throughout this journey have been invaluable.

I am also especially grateful to Jennifer Lévy for her beautiful work and for her companionship on the road; to Dania Davey for her tireless and creative input in pulling this all together and for understanding each woman's space so effortlessly; to Barbara Marks for her never-ending enthusiasm, suggestions, and friendship; and to Dianne Hudson and Ellen Rakieten for being steady believers in this project.

To everyone at Clarkson Potter, especially to Alberto Vitale, Lauren Shakely, Chip Gibson, Joan Denman, Maggie Hinders, Andrew Martin, Mark McCauslin, Mary Ellen Briggs, Joan De Mayo, John Son, and Laurie Stark, many thanks.

Special gratitude to my terrific assistants, past and present, who always pour on the energy for me: Juli Grossfield, Barbara Muller, Julie Maher, Donna Mollica, and Celeste Sissons.

Thanks to the "Seven Sisters"—Nancy, Jannie, Donna, Jerrilee, Mouse, Becky, and Kathy—for their friendship and nonjudgmental support during the especially hectic times; to my own sisters, Mary and Jeanne; and to my brothers, Tom, John, Jim, Justin, and Paul.

To my support group of healing people—Sam Schwartz, Andrew Gentile, David Lawrence, Bernard Raxlen, Betty Iacono, Bruce Yaffe, Sylvana Stein, Marc Lowenberg, Soham, June, Sue, Giselle, Kim, and Terry Iacuso—all of you help me stay together, body and soul.

And to those special places that renew my spirit—10,000 Waves, The New Age Health Spa, The Norwich Spa, The Chateau Elan.

Thank you to those who found time in their busy lives to advise and counsel me: Nan and Norm Rosenblatt, Nancy Novograd, Frank Newbold, Deborah Parsons, Susan Finklestein, Anne Keating, Mike Strohl, Toni Gallagher, Sissy and Bob Eagan, Stephanie Fisher-Zernin, Alix McLean, Judy Auchincloss, May Nakib, Francis Mason, Sharne Algotsson, Denys Davis, Michell Waldron, Jeffrey Bilhuber, Cheryl Masur, Gioietta Vitale, Bridget Marmion, Jill Cohen, Susan DuPape, Rochelle Udell, and Judy Daniels.

To the many women I've met along this journey whose names I neglected to mention, thank you.

And a special thanks to my late grandmothers, Mamie Hill and Grandma Casson, who taught me the secret of magic places that could take me away.

acknowledgments

contents

"What is the answer? There is no easy answer, no complete answer. I have only clues, shells from the sea. The bare beauty of the channeled whelk tells me that one answer, and perhaps a first step, is in simplification of life, in cutting out some of the distractions. But how? Total retirement is not possible. I cannot shed my responsibilities. I cannot permanently inhabit a desert island. I cannot be a nun in the midst of a family life. I would not want to be. The solution for me, surely, is neither in total renunciation of the world, nor in total acceptance of it. I must find a balance somewhere, or an alternating rhythm between these two extremes; a swinging of the pendulum between solitude and communion, between retreat and return. In my periods of retreat, perhaps I can learn something to carry back into my worldly life, as a beginning. I can follow this superficial clue, and see where it leads. Here, I can try."

—ANNE MORROW LINDBERGH, <u>Gifts from the Sea</u>

This book, my eleventh, has been an incredible and absolutely essential journey for me. Like so many members of my generation, I have over the years grown into a life full of opportunities and options that my mother and grandmothers could only have dreamed of. For those of us women who came of age as part of the Baby Boom, the cultural message has been not only could we do it all, but why not do it all! Yet as exhilarating and fulfilling as this has been for me, it has also come with its downside—the loss of a private time and space for myself.

11

In speaking with many women across the country, I have discovered that as much as we revel in the hard-won victories that have given us new freedoms in pursuing careers and in creating loving relationships, many of us long to find the time in our busy schedules to relax and refresh ourselves, body and spirit. All the requisite aspects of life on the cusp of a new century have made it difficult (let's be honest—almost impossible!) to have some time alone, especially if we have others who depend on us.

One of the most intriguing facts I discovered while doing research for my book *Bathrooms,* was that 46 percent of American women say that their favorite mode of relaxation is to take a bath. I'm firmly convinced that we retreat to the tub to savor a few quiet moments—however brief—of sanctuary and personal time. Baths are about quietude as much as they are about cleanliness. Here we can, if only momentarily, shut out the world and all its demands.

Reflecting on what I was hearing from the women I spoke with, I was reminded of a pervasive theme that resonates in Anne Morrow Lindbergh's exquisitely written little book, *Gifts from the Sea*. Lindbergh was married to the adventurer and American hero, Charles Lindbergh, and was raising five children when she wrote, "What a curious act we women perform everyday of our lives. It puts the trapeze artists to shame. Look at us. We run a tightrope daily, balancing a pile of books on the head. Baby carriages, parasol, kitchen, chair, still under control. Steady now!"

Lindbergh goes on to reflect, in words that could be uttered with absolute relevance today, "The problem is how to remain whole in the midst of the distractions of life; how to remain balanced, no matter what shocks come in at the periphery and tend to crack the hub of the wheel. For to be a woman is to have interests and duties, ranging out in all directions from the central mother-core, like spokes from the hub of a wheel."

Lindbergh's words suggest that we would not be spoiling ourselves if we gave ourselves the gifts of time and space, those elements that create the "balance beam" of life. I firmly believe that in order to give back to our

relationships, careers, families, and passions, we must pull in for short moments to take care of ourselves; then we can return to the people and places of our lives renewed, refreshed, and ready to continue the drama of our days with all the joys, sorrows, pleasures, and stresses that go with it. The simplicity of listening to a favorite CD, the calmness of soaking in a hot bath, the ease of resting on a bench at the edge of a garden: these personal spaces feed our souls, allowing us to restore our spirits and enjoy our lives. Although Virginia Woolf writes that a woman must have money and a room of her own if she is to write fiction, I believe a woman today must have a room of her own if she is to survive and thrive.

I unearthed some wonderful personal spaces in my journey, from Ali MacGraw's small studio in northern New Mexico with its incredible mountain views, where she finds "silence and tranquillity," to designer Sherri Donghia's fabric-filled loft in her Long Island country home, where she can "stop and think and relax, to be really honest and creative," to television commentator Chantal Westerman's Hollywood home, where, amid a collection of altars, crosses, and other religious icons, she has created a "sacred place," a peaceful and serene sanctuary.

The spaces that Jennifer Lévy and I photographed for *A Room of Her Own* came in all shapes, sizes, and venues. For fashion designer Adrienne Vittadini, it was a small pool house elegantly suggesting a miniature classical temple. For museum curator Dianne Pilgrim, it was the corner of her New York apartment with its collection of favorite decorative arts objects, and its first-rate view of the city skyline; for L.A. designer Lynn von Kersting, it was a romantic

oval sitting room, while for author and mountain climber Sandy Hill, it was a Tibetan tent pitched on the lawn of her Connecticut home and filled with mementos and found objects.

And the connective thread for all of these "personal spaces" is that each one, in dazzlingly different ways, brings its owner the sense of solitude, of sanctuary they need in their rich and engaged lives. Amid the diversity, there were some elements that I found repeated often, such things as glorious fabric and pillows, baskets and bird nests, stones, altars, photographs, and row upon row of hats, boats, books, and shells. Music, scented candles, and views of nature were also important elements in these zones of privacy.

In perusing these pages, I hope you too will find inspiration and ideas that can apply to your life. And may we all find the time and courage to claim a bit of personal space of our own. I wish you well!

CELEBRATING COLOR

DENISE DUMMONT   ANNA BELLA CHAPMAN

SHERRI DONGHIA ELLA KING TORREY BARBARA BULLOCK BEATRICE WOOD

Tropical Nuances

Born in Brazil, Denise Dummont is an actress, singer, and translator who lives in New York City with her husband, Matthew Chapman, an English film director and screenwriter, and their two children, Diego Antonio and Anna Bella. Dummont has lived in the United States since 1984 but still keeps an apartment in Rio de Janeiro. "My whole life has been sort of split between south and north of the equator," she says. "I went to school in Brazil, but college in New York, and my work has taken me all over the world."

After a stint in Los Angeles, home now is a sprawling apartment overlooking New York's East River. Her personal space there is the library of the apartment, which has a superb view of the river. "It's certainly my favorite room and where I spend a lot of time," she notes. "It's where most of my treasures are—my books, scripts, records, films, photos, my shell collections. It's a place where I study my scripts and plays, do translations, practice my singing, rehearse, watch movies, read, nap, or just daydream."

ABOVE: Denise Dummont in her New York library overlooking the East River. BELOW: A collection of boxes, created with her daughter, Anna Bella, made from shells gathered on the beaches of Brazil. OPPOSITE: Wrought-iron garden chairs, splashed with an array of colorful cushions, evoke Dummont's Brazilian background and her California garden.

21

Sunlight pouring through the windows is tempered by bamboo green walls that overflow with Dummont's huge collection of books and records, as well as her husband's more academic works. Music plays a big part in her life: Dummont's father, Humberto Teixeira, was one of Brazil's leading composers in the 1950s (some of his songs were recorded by Carmen Miranda), and her mother, Margarida Jatoba, was an actress and is now a classical pianist.

A rough-hewn, green painted table is surrounded by chairs from her old garden in California and provides a work area, while an old red-and-white plaid sofa is cherished for its comfort. The sofa reminds Dummont of Brazil. "For me," she says, "this color combination is very Brazilian; these are the colors of my country." In general, the library is "a mixture of Portuguese and English, Victorian and contemporary, and definitely tropical as well."

The mélange of objects reflects Dummont's personal and professional lives, from a bowl of seashells she collected with her daughter on a visit to Brazil, to CDs of her father's recordings, to mementos from some of the films she has made. "I try to be neat," Dummont says with a laugh, "and having such a full space, I have to be. Otherwise, one wouldn't be able to walk through here! But neatness is not my main concern. After all, I am Brazilian and as we say down there, 'there's no sin below the equator.'

"But this is a very inspiring place for me," she continues, "and not just because of the objects, but because of the view of the water and the bridges . . . the continual sense of motion and activity. I love this space because I can close the doors and be by myself, or open them and have delicious dinner parties with my family and friends around the table."

The sun-drenched red-and-white plaid sofa is from Denise Dummont's guest house in California. She had bookcases built to hold her extensive and eclectic collection of books.

23

A Child's Room

At age eight, Anna Bella Chapman has very definitive ideas about her personal space and what it means to her. The daughter of Denise Dummont (see page 21), she lives with her mother and father, Matthew Chapman, in their New York City apartment. Anna Bella has determined that her private space is her bedroom. "I like it," she says, "because it has all the things I grew up with, like Pinky Bear, my first teddy bear, and because no one can come in here without my permission."

Like her mother, Anna Bella gets enormous pleasure from the apartment's view of the tugboats on the East River. Her lace-draped canopy bed is her favorite place, complete with a "dream catcher" hanging down from the canopy. Here she can read, snuggle up with her dog, Gracie, and occasionally take a flying leap into the air.

A small, pink, handmade mailbox is perched on the entryway wall to the room, waiting to receive messages and private notes, a very proper-looking pink dollhouse sits on her desk, and a wide bookcase holds her vast assemblage of dolls and books. Surrounded by her favorite things, Anna Bella, at an early age, has discovered the joys of a private place.

TOP: *A floral-topped lamp shares space with Anna Bella's beloved dollhouse on a crowded desk.*
ABOVE: *A simple wooden mailbox for messages is an essential part of Anna Bella's room.*
OPPOSITE: *Flying through the air, Anna Bella exudes joy on her lace-draped bed.*

Loft Visions

Sherri Donghia is passionate about her private retreat in the country. "Since it's on the top floor of my home," she says, "it is truly private—off limits even to house guests." For this is where Donghia not only retreats from her weekday world but also where she gathers ideas for her ever-evolving collections of textiles.

As vice president of design and marketing for Donghia Furniture and Textiles, she has played a major role in directing the fortunes of the firm founded in 1968 by her brother, the late Angelo Donghia; the company has established its name designing timeless furniture and fabrics for the home. Over the years, Donghia has sought out beautiful textiles, beads, and objects from around the world while traveling with her husband, who is a fashion executive. Today, many of these items are displayed in and around her balcony studio.

"This room reflects my many years of collecting," she explains. "More than the rest of my house it's become my main area both for storing and displaying my collections. I love the primitive and the exotic, and I love having handmade baskets, boxes, and bags to put all my things into. I display all these 'works in progress' here so they can inspire me."

For Donghia, there is no set time of the day or night that is put aside for herself. "Whenever I pass by and

TOP: *Old and new family members line the shelf on a studio wall.*
ABOVE: *Sherri Donghia in her private loft.*
OPPOSITE: *A handful of primitive beads and ethnic fabrics give Donghia inspiration for her work and her life.*

have a few minutes," she says, "I try to stop in. I keep things easily accessible so I can find time to recharge, relax, or start planning a new project." Often reevaluating her space to see how "livable and comfortable it is," Donghia isn't timid about rearranging it to keep it both timely and timeless. The room becomes a kind of movable feast in that she uses many of her found treasures to adorn both herself and the other rooms in her home. She says, "Your home should be constantly evolving, I think. Not everything has to last forever."

But her private loft always draws her back. "It is a place to think and relax, to be really honest and creative with the precious moments alone I have all too few of these days!"

LEFT: Although small and narrow (9½ by 15 feet), her attic studio is filled with the relics of Donghia's travels. RIGHT, TOP TO BOTTOM: Small, elegant touches imbue the room with personality.

OVERLEAF, LEFT: A close-up detail of Donghia's corkboard. RIGHT: A second private place—an inviting hammock nestled in her backyard forest of pine.

29

Passions and Places

"In one form or another, this room has been with me for decades," says Ella King Torrey, the president of the San Francisco Art Institute, speaking of the sitting room in her home in San Francisco. "I have been reinventing it and adding to it every time I move, but it remains fundamentally the same."

Torrey's journey to the San Francisco Art Institute, where she is responsible for the long-range plans of one of the premier colleges of art in the country, led through such diverse points as the Center for the Study of Southern Culture in Oxford, Mississippi, the Whitney Museum in New York, and the Harvard Theatre Collection in Cambridge, Massachusetts. A graduate of Yale and the University of Mississippi, Torrey is trained as an art historian with a specialty in American folk and popular art.

ABOVE: Ella King Torrey in her sitting room.
BELOW: A corner detail of a needlepoint pillow.
OPPOSITE: A detail of the vibrantly colored "hand" quilt crafted by Sarah Mary Taylor, an artist from Yazoo City, Mississippi.

33

"This room is an accumulation of twenty-five years of passions and places," Torrey says. "A Victorian couch bought at a Salvation Army store when I was fifteen years old; quilts by black women from Mississippi; carvings from Africa, Guatemala, and Indonesia; contemporary art by artists from Philadelphia; and a rug woven by a Berber woman as a blanket for her

family." Regardless of their origin, all of these collected objects share, in Torrey's eyes, "an exuberance of color and shape and form" that inspires her. "In this space," she explains, "I seek to surround myself with joy. Every object here is connected to a personal place or experience of great importance to me, and so sitting here surrounded by my history helps keep me whole."

Torrey tends to gravitate toward this room for "transition times—those moments on the weekend morning when I'm having coffee and planning the day, or the time in the evening when I am just home and regrouping before I go out again. I don't usually work here; I just relax and think. This room really feeds my soul and reminds me of life's wonderful possibilities."

ABOVE LEFT: A stool found in Cameroon, West Africa, serves as an end table.
LEFT: Two prototype wood chairs by designer Agnes Bourne.
RIGHT: A Victorian sofa, discovered by Torrey at a Salvation Army store at age fifteen, finds a fresh life in the midst of newer acquisitions in her colorful sitting room.

Kitchen Art

"I love kitchens," says Philadelphia artist Barbara Bullock. "It's the one room that always seems to contain good things to eat, comfortable chairs, and great smells." A prolific painter whose work has been shown widely (her collage *Releasing the Energies Balances the Spirit* is installed in the Philadelphia International Airport), Bullock has filled her kitchen with found objects and with the textiles and colors that she loves.

ABOVE: *Barbara Bullock in her kitchen.*
OPPOSITE: *Spirit House, an exuberant piece by Bullock created from watercolor paper and acrylic paint, dominates one wall of her kitchen.*

"My kitchen is like one of my paintings," she notes. "The difference is that I can move around in it. And I love my collection of old dishes, these plates and platters shaped like fruits and vegetables that all have a history." Hot peppers, dried plants, and garlic hang on the walls, and bags of beans (black, lima, red, and pinto), olive oil, and seasonings are abundantly displayed, creating vibrant vignettes throughout the room.

"I love to hang my art up in the kitchen—here I seem to see it for the first time," says Bullock, whose paintings feature African tribal motifs, rituals, and symbols. "I painted my chairs and the other furniture in the kitchen with soft Santa Fe colors and attached animal sculpture to the chairs, with seashells, scarabs from Egypt, and African designs."

Bullock's kitchen is an intense reflection of her interest in African arts and crafts. A tableau created on one shelf displays a carving of an African woman with a beatific smile on her face; she holds two babies and has an animated dog at her feet. A sunflower dish stands behind her and a carved banana tree is next to her. "I love looking at that scene," muses Bullock.

Objects with personal history and meaning permeate the kitchen: a small pillow crafted by one of her students that rests in a bamboo chair at the kitchen window, Mexican pottery collected on her travels, a Zebra pot purchased in Ghana. Bullock had no special plan, no grand scheme in creating this very personal space. "I believe it simply happened," she says. "I think that a good kitchen just calls you to it."

LEFT: Melon dessert bowls form a colorful still life.
RIGHT: One of Bullock's students created the raspberry pillow on the bamboo chair in her kitchen.

A Jeweled Tableau

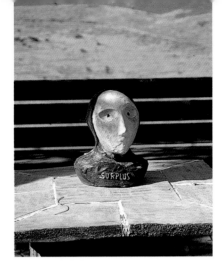

"There are three things important in life: honesty, which means living free of the cunning of the mind; compassion, because if we have no concern for others, we are monsters; and curiosity, for if the mind is not searching, it is dull and unresponsive," declares Beatrice Wood, who, at 104 years of age, is still infinitely curious, compassionate, and honest. She is also a real treasure, having been designated a "Living Treasure of the State of California" by Governor Pete Wilson in 1994, and an "Esteemed Living Artist" by the Smithsonian Institution.

Today, atop a mountain in Ojai, California, where she lives and works—she creates in her studio every single day—Wood can look back on a fulfilling career as a gifted potter who also has lived an exceptionally adventurous life: first, as a rebellious young woman who escaped her conventional Park Avenue family to join a theater group in Paris at the age of seventeen and, later, as an artist who went on to become a regular in the bohemian salons surrounding the New York Dada group. "I always wanted to run away from home," Wood recalls. "I was brought up in quite a good deal of comfort with a governess. My parents were very generous; my father was in real estate and my mother wanted me

TOP: Beatrice Wood's Surplus, *which she created in 1950, sits on her terrace amidst the Ojai mountains.*
ABOVE: The spirited artist on her 100th birthday.
OPPOSITE: Anaïs Nin once said of Wood's gold lusterware, "To drink water from a goblet by Beatrice Wood changes it to wine."

OVERLEAF: A lifetime of art and artifacts created and collected by Wood fills her living room.

to marry a stockbroker. Of course, I was in great rebellion."

After trying her hand at acting, she became involved with the art world of the early 1920s, as well as with the Dada movement, and entered into a relationship with the painter Marcel Duchamp. Wood insists her natural gifts for painting and drawing were limited. "I was more or less encouraged to draw and paint, which I've always done, although I've never taken my abilities too seriously."

Beato, as she is known, has always felt she has no technique—only moods.

Her interest in pottery was ignited, she says, "by accident." On a trip to Holland in 1929, she bought a half-dozen lusterware plates for her upcoming marriage. The wedding was canceled, but she continued to hunt for the right teapot to match her plates; in frustration, she decided to take a pottery course at Hollywood High School and make it herself. She was unable to produce the teapot, but this exhilarating experience introduced Wood to the world of pottery.

More courses and apprenticeships followed and eventually she settled in Ojai, California, on a one-square-acre "rock pile" where she set up her home and studio. "Ojai was the pot of gold at the end of a long, obstacle-strewn rainbow," she says. "From the moment that I arrived on March 3, 1948, time ceased." And it was here in Ojai that Wood established her reputation as a gifted potter, admired especially for her luster glazes.

Shown at work at her glaze table in the documentary about her, *The Mama of Dada,* Wood explains, "What I do is cook—a little of this . . . a little of that."

If her studio is her space of creation, then her candy-colored living/sitting room is her personal space of relaxation. Walls, floors, baskets, shelves, bookcases, and chairs all glow with the rich palette of her life, creating a jewel-like effect night and day. Lining one wall are some remarkable examples of paintings on glass from India, collected during her visits to that country. An acid-yellow, L-shaped sectional sofa is piled high with the pillows she has collected throughout her life (including one from Rudolph Valentino's bed!). It's backed by a sari-draped bookcase that is used not only for books but also to display her one-of-a-kind works of art.

On the other side of the room sits a soft peach bergère in a Fortuny-esque fabric. From this comfortable spot, she gazes out at the Ojai mountains, where, Wood says, she can see "a beautiful shady place under a wonderful protective tree. Here, in this space, I never feel isolated from nature and the beauty of life."

LEFT: An oxblood chest from Wood's mother showcases her collection of Buddhas.
RIGHT: A Spanish chest holds more treasures next to a face mask of Wood.

OVERLEAF, LEFT: A peek at Wood's outdoor "throne," created by Gail Cottman and consisting of cement, beads, and shards of Wood's creations.
RIGHT: Three shimmering lusterware bottles created by Beatrice Wood in the mid-1960s.

SACRED
PLACES

CAROL AND ELAINE ANTHONY

CHANTAL WESTERMAN

SALLY QUINN

SISTER MARY JOAQUIN

ALI MacGRAW

Spirited Echoes

Carol Anthony and Elaine Anthony are twin sisters and best friends; both are also highly acclaimed artists. Their works have been widely exhibited throughout the country and were shown together for the first time at a joint exhibition at the Neuberger Museum of Art in Purchase, New York, in the winter of 1996. Entitled "Shared Beginnings/Separate Passages: Retrospective Exhibitions of the Work of Carol Anthony and Elaine Anthony," the show opened to unanimous acclaim.

Although their work differs in approach and sensibility, the shared visual themes—whimsical sculpture, architectural ruins, collages, scraps of letters and postcards—are a testimony to the mystery of twinness. "Our paintings are souvenirs of memories and unspoken comments—dreams that have already transpired—the remains of a cracked shell," said Carol recently.

Carol and Elaine grew up in New York City and Greenwich, Connecticut, in an exuberantly creative family. "Ours was a childhood filled with music, singing, athletics, arts and crafts, hobby shows, and an overwhelming spirit of adventure," Elaine remembers. Their father was the creative director of the Young and Rubicam advertising agency and a cartoon contributor to *The New Yorker* magazine; their mother came from a

ABOVE: Looking like a tiny Norwegian house, yet nestled in the winter woods of Connecticut, the guest house where Elaine Anthony can sit surrounded by her own and her children's artwork.
BELOW: A photograph of Carol Anthony's adobe sanctuary is propped up on a ledge near her fireplace.
OPPOSITE: Elaine and Carol working together, and obviously enjoying their joint effort in producing some lithographs.

51

TOP LEFT AND ABOVE LEFT: Details of Elaine's found objects and art.
TOP RIGHT: Carol's assemblage of carefully chosen and symbolic pieces.
ABOVE RIGHT: A luminous egg painted by Carol on a cookie sheet.
OPPOSITE: A close-up of Carol's thatch-topped sanctuario.

OVERLEAF, LEFT: Carol's altar of special objects, with a kiva blazing in the corner.
RIGHT: A close-up of one of Carol's painting.

musical/theatrical background and had performed off-Broadway, with her own two sisters. Carol recalls: "Elaine and I were brought up in a very crazy and loving family of artists, musicians, and cartoonists. . . . I fell in love with that whole rich life."

Echoes Elaine, "We lived in a world of total creativity. Carol and I would learn songs from all the Broadway hits and we sang and danced."

Together, the sisters attended Stevens College, a small two-year college, and then, as both had always planned, began their serious study of art at the Rhode Island School of Design. From there, their careers have followed separate but parallel paths, with each utilizing different techniques and materials but exhibiting strong similarities in content, particularly in their intense focus on the importance of "sacred spaces." As Carol observes, "We are both always attracted to the same kinds of people, to the spirit within, to altars, rituals . . ." Similarly, Elaine refers to the significance of the Catholic Church, the "idea of cloisters, silent temples, silent churches . . . that sense of silent, reverent spaces."

Interestingly, the sisters live thousands of miles apart, Carol in the desert outside Santa Fe, New Mexico, and Elaine in the bucolic village of West

Redding, Connecticut.

Carol settled outside of Santa Fe in 1992 and created there a private sanctuary, the Strawbale Cloister, as "a slice of eighteenth-century time, frozen." Her studio and home, which she describes as her "cloistered clustered *casita* and sanctuary," is nestled in a hillside studded with "pinion, juniper, gamma grass, chamisa, and arroyos."

Here she finds inspiration for her images of timeless landscapes and magical rooms. "My private space is my home and my land," Carol observes. "Here is where I hold the presence of the unknown—its light, its sweetness, its calm, its mystery, and its ability to nourish and free us."

The adobe-walled living room where Carol recharges after eight- to ten-hour days in her studio is filled with her creations, and with the antiques and found objects she has gathered over the years. The coffee table is piled high with art books and catalogs, and laden with her own luminescently painted boxes and her collections of rocks, feathers, and birds' nests. A deep sofa is covered in a durable chocolate brown fabric— the ideal "kick back" spot at the end of the day.

Just outside this room, her *santuario,* or "shrine"— a thatched-domed adobe structure surrounded by sage brush and aspen trees —is where Carol retreats

ABOVE: *Carol's* Pignon Field
Box *was created on the top of a
cigar box.*
RIGHT: Black Mesa Studies *was
executed by Elaine in 1987.*

to rekindle the strength she derives from her beloved New Mexico landscape. In the small hut, with its altar niche bearing a candle constantly lit in homage to her sister, Carol finds solitude and strength.

Back east, in Connecticut, Elaine Anthony lives and paints and creates her assemblages and collage work in a turreted white studio in her home several hours from New York.

Elaine, like her twin, has several personal spaces. One is a cozy little Scandinavian guest house designed by her husband, well-known architect Bernard Wharton. The living area of the guest cottage is an idyllic retreat, with its soft leather sofa and club chair, and its chalk white walls covered with her large-scale paintings and Mexican artifacts.

Her other sanctuary is a votive candle–filled porch

LEFT: Elaine's artwork propped against the walls next to the stone fireplace.
RIGHT: A front view of the same fireplace, which was created from rocks found on the property.

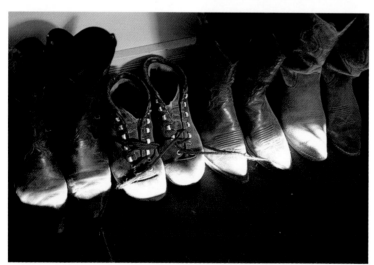

with well-worn wicker, comfortable pillows, and an altar she created on her fiftieth birthday. Surrounded by breathtaking views of the Connecticut countryside, the porch resembles a cross between a Russian dacha and an Adirondack camp, with red brick laid in a herringbone pattern, and cedar shakes lining the walls.

"I have various personal spaces and each carries a different energy that I need for my head and my heart," Elaine says. Reflecting upon these spaces, she echoes her twin in saying, "I don't know how we would survive without personal sanctuaries. We have our souls to care for, after all!"

TOP: *Assorted boots in Elaine's household in Connecticut.*
CENTER LEFT: *A private moment for Elaine in front of one of her much-loved bonfires.*
CENTER RIGHT: *Carol and her dogs peek out of her straw bale* sanctuario.
BOTTOM: *Carol's footwear in Santa Fe.*
RIGHT: *A large refectory table is perpendicular to a moving sculpture created by Elaine's son, Pedro.*

A Spiritual Place

As the Hollywood correspondent for ABC-TV's *Good Morning America,* Chantal Westerman leads a whirlwind professional life. In addition to interviewing scores of American entertainment figures, she has traveled to Australian islands to interview aborigines and to Spain to preview Seville's new opera house with Placido Domingo.

Westerman's interview with actor Michael Landon discussing his battle with cancer was cited by the Museum of Television and Radio as one of the best interviews of the decade. She is also an active supporter of charities, from the Shoulder, a shelter for recovering alcoholic women in Houston, to Project Angel Food, which provides meals to AIDS patients in Los Angeles.

Home is Hollywood, where she lives with her two cats, Smoke and Rudy, and her dog, Millie. In her bright top-floor apartment with its tree-level view, Westerman has created a personal retreat for herself, a decidedly spiritual, as opposed to religious, sanctuary that is far removed from the fast-paced world she covers for ABC-TV.

In this room, a collection of crosses of varying sizes hangs on the wall overlooking a desk topped by several religious icons. Against another wall, votive candles flank

ABOVE: Chantal Westerman in her retreat.
OPPOSITE: A sea of crosses creates a still life on a wall in Westerman's Los Angeles apartment.

a statue of the Blessed Virgin draped with rosary beads. Still another and more elaborate altar anchors yet another wall in the room.

"To me," Westerman says, "a personal space is about peacefulness and serenity. The crosses and altars make me feel safe and spiritual." She recalls that "someone once told me a long time ago that organized religion is for people who are afraid they will go to hell. Spirituality is for those of us who have

already been there . . . and actually, I qualify."

In this "sacred space," Westerman finds sanctuary and renewal. "My life is so filled with activity—people, phone calls, schedules, airlines—that I can't really meditate at a designated time. Instead, my body and my brain will suddenly say, 'STOP!' to me. It's astonishing because I listen. I stop, turn off the phones, and sit."

Creating a "comfort zone," as Westerman puts it, need not be an expen-

sive proposition. The key, she says, is "to make it conducive to curling up—I've collected lots of chenille throws, blankets, and comforters. Stillness is very soothing to me, and when I walk in here, it simply envelops me."

ABOVE: Two wooden angels preside over the living room, which resonates with quiet spirituality.
OPPOSITE, ABOVE: A rush settee is a stage for favorite books and memorabilia, a framed print, and a photo of Westerman and her dog.
OPPOSITE, BELOW: A butler's tray table holds personal mementos: horns, snuff bottles, and several pieces from her extensive collection of crosses and religious artifacts.

A Thatched Haven

"Women are responsible for so many things today, for so many people . . . we seem to have time to nurture everyone but ourselves. Often we give away the best of what we have to everyone else and save nothing for us. A private place helps us to get back, retrieve and re-create what we have bestowed on others—even if we're just going to go back out and give it away again. It's awfully refreshing and energizing to be able to say 'What about me!' for a change."

This is Sally Quinn, author, journalist, and doyenne of the Washington political and social scene, musing on her hideaway. It's a thatched-roof cottage tucked away in the garden of Grey Gardens, her Long Island summer home and the subject of a much-praised documentary that examined its extraordinary past as the home of Jacqueline Kennedy Onassis's eccentric relatives and their many cats.

When she decorated the small space, Quinn says, she wanted it to be "a throwback to the turn of the century when the cottage was built." She added a wicker sofa with faded linen cushions, several rag rugs, a throw, old books, candles, a rustic mirror, and oil paintings, "all lending an atmosphere of coziness, a place which looked like it had always been there," she explains.

TOP: *Sally Quinn in her cottage.* ABOVE: *Reading a deck of tarot cards.*
OPPOSITE: *Surrounded by the lush greenery and foliage of Grey Gardens, Quinn's turn-of-the-century cottage offers total sanctuary.*

OVERLEAF, LEFT: *The pale painted wicker furniture captures the feeling of an earlier time.* RIGHT: *A detail of the garden wall.*

The small cottage is situated a comfortable distance from the main house and, most important for Quinn, does not have a telephone. "It's so quiet and peaceful," she observes, "with just the sound of the waves against the shore on the other side of the hedges. When my son was a baby, I would come down here to nurse him in private. It was a magical time for both of us."

Quinn's cozy cottage has a lived-in ambience. "I like a little clutter," she notes, "and things that are messed up a bit. I like spaces that feel lived in, as though a human person has actually been there. Perfection and total neatness give me the creeps."

The cottage most definitely has the owner's personal stamp on it: books, flowers, mementos collected on travels, shells brought in from the beach, treasures found at flea markets, a handmade pottery dish from her son, and photographs of the family.

"I'm a big believer in personalizing my surroundings," she notes. In recent years, Quinn has begun to read tarot cards and palms. "The cottage is a wonderful place to do that," she says with a smile. "Grey Gardens is haunted anyway, so a little occult activity seems appropriate."

ABOVE: A natural ceiling of hanging plants creates a quiet refuge in a corner of the garden. RIGHT: Peegee hydrangeas form a gracious canopy around Adirondack chairs.

A Simple Sanctuary

The land surrounding Sister Mary Joaquin's tiny adobe home in the northern New Mexican desert seems to resound with the spirit of the ancient Anasazi Indians who lie buried between the stark mesas and arroyos.

Reachable only by miles of dirt road and without electricity or telephones, the Christ in the Desert Monastery is not a usual destination for visitors to Santa Fe. But for Sister Joaquin, as she is known, Santa Fe was only a stopover (albeit one for almost thirty years) on her journey to a contemplative life at the monastery, where a Benedictine order of monks follows the cycle of labor and prayer that they have practiced since the sixth century. In fact, she had been coming out here on weekends many years earlier to "recharge" while she was running Saint Vincent's Hospital in Santa Fe.

Born seventy-four years ago in Ohio, Sister Joaquin studied nursing and as a young woman became interested in the American Sisters of Charity. She joined the order, completed her nursing training, and eventually settled in Santa Fe, where she had an active career as a builder and as chief executive officer of Saint Vincent's Hospital. It was during the early years there, she recalls, "with meetings from six A.M. to midnight, that I began coming out here to the monastery on the weekends just to get away from the

TOP: *Blue sky, mesas, and the Chama River frame Sister Mary Joaquin's simple dwelling.*
CENTER: *Our Lady of Mount Carmel scapular on the desk blotter.*
BOTTOM: *A rock nestled in the stone garden outside Sister Joaquin's home.*
OPPOSITE: *Sister Joaquin on her meditation log, surrounded by the Sangre de Cristo mountains.*

hospital rat race. I'd return to work on Monday feeling completely new!"

Over time, Sister Joaquin began to search for a different way to express her vocation. Eventually she resigned from Saint Vincent's and joined her old friend Father Aelred in Mexico, where she ran a family clinic for twelve years near the Rio Bravo. After his death, Sister Joaquin was invited by the Benedictine monks of Christ in the Desert Monastery to live in a small adobe dwelling on the edge of their property.

Her days are simple. Living as a hermit, she spends most of her time in prayer. She rises at 3:30 in the morning and travels a half mile to join the brothers for the first morning

LEFT: A handmade throw covers a rocking chair in the small (10 by 10 foot) bedroom.
TOP RIGHT: A collection of religious artifacts lines the walls leading to Sister Joaquin's bedroom.
CENTER RIGHT: Our Lady of Vladimer, a Russian icon, hangs over her bed.
BOTTOM RIGHT: A serene corner desk is where Sister Joaquin communicates by letter with outsiders as part of her ministry.

ABOVE LEFT: A seven-day candle on a small dresser.
ABOVE RIGHT: Heat in the harsh New Mexican winters is provided by a wood-burning stove. A Benedictine monk created the icon of St. John the Baptist hanging above.
OPPOSITE: The simplicity of the Benedictine life is reflected in this view of Sister Joaquin's doorway.

prayer—Lauds—which is one of the seven hours of the Divine Office sung in chant each day. Later, she shares lunch with them in silence. The rest of her day is spent in prayer and solitude.

Her adobe-and-wood dwelling consists of a bath, small kitchen, and bedroom. "Since simplicity and poverty are what a religious strives for all his or her life," Sister Joaquin explains, "there was not much 'decorating' to do."

The scents of pinon and sage from a wood-burning stove permeate her ten-foot-square bedroom. A wooden desk holds her few possessions, including her books and weekday missal, writing paper, an old letter scale, stamps, matches, and a flashlight. A framed sepia-toned photograph of Saint Thérèse of Lisieux hangs near her wooden locker; a seven-day candle stands on a chest of drawers. The plaster walls hold various religious icons, some from past trips to Greece, and her single bed is covered with a muted plaid throw.

"Prayer can be just giving yourself a quiet little space," Sister Joaquin explains. "I didn't search for this particular place. It was here and the brothers offered it to me. I love the smallness of it—it's very livable."

Outside, with a view of the Chama River and the surrounding red sandstone cliffs, is Sister Joaquin's open-air retreat: a small wooden bench made from a tree trunk. Stretching beyond is the harsh, beautiful expanse of the New Mexican desert—the sand-blown sagebrush, the dusty chamisa, and the pale rocks and boulders that border the sliver of the flowing river. The calmness of her space is all-encompassing.

Gentle Meditation

When Ali MacGraw—actress, author, and creator of a best-selling yoga videotape—bought her home, tucked away in a valley in northern New Mexico, she immediately hired a local architect to work with her in building a small studio adjacent to but separate from the main house. MacGraw recalls, "I liked the idea of a certain separation between my 'real house' and a space in which I could find silence and tranquillity. I wanted to be able to turn off the phones,

and perhaps even leave my two dogs and two cats 'home' so that I could work or do yoga with absolutely no distraction."

Working with the architect, her primary objective was to make the space as efficient as possible. "I put in a proper bathroom with a shower and a survival kitchen," she notes. "The decoration is terribly minimal and more

LEFT: *On an outer wall of the adobe house is a small opening with favorite objects and artifacts.*
ABOVE: *Ali MacGraw in her studio, practicing yoga.*
OPPOSITE: *A stepstool leads to the raised pillow-laden bed niche that MacGraw carved into one wall of her studio.*

about function than any-
thing else." A kiva fireplace
was added, as well as a simple worktable topped by
a handcrafted mica lamp.
Painted Shaker pegs are
everywhere. "They are simple and beautiful and serve to
hang everything from soggy
winter clothes to some of
my favorite flea market finds,
like African beads to be
strung into necklaces."

MacGraw has always
saved ethnic textiles and
jewelry, and what decora-
tion there is in the studio
reflects these collections. A
faded dhurrie rug in shades
of celadon, peach, and
chocolate brown provides
a serene and comfortable
spot for her daily yoga, and
beeswax candles through-
out the room accentuate
the gentle ambience.

A queen-sized bed—
flanked by built-in book-
shelves and elevated to take
advantage of an incredible
view toward the mountains—

*LEFT: A bejeweled mannequin is a
resting place for some of MacGraw's
treasured pieces and bags.*
*RIGHT: Cherished mementos, from
horseshoes, beads, and personal
papers to a small painting by her
mother, crown the desk area beneath
the mica lamp.*

doubles, says MacGraw, "as a big squashy sitting area." She has left the rest of the room sparsely furnished because she uses it for yoga and meditation.

"Most everything I have in this space is very personal," she explains. "There are lots of photographs of my son, my friends, our animals, mementos from my travels, wildflowers, found rocks and bits from my walks in the arroyo." Many souvenirs of her son's childhood were lost in the Malibu, California, fires in 1993, but the few that remain—like his handprint at age three—are here in the studio.

"I think all of us, men and women, need a tiny spot of total privacy, of stillness, to reconnect with our own souls," MacGraw says. "I know that the ability to regenerate, to get away a bit, enhances not only my mental health but my ability to work and create and, probably, to navigate the complicated relationships that make up the rest of my life."

Catty-corner to the bed niche is a kiva fireplace with a wide sitting ledge.

SANDY HILL

CHARLOTTE MOSS

GLENNA GOODACRE

OPRAH WINFREY

VICTORIA MacKENZIE-CHILDS

HELEN BALLARD WEEKS

WORKING
SANCTUARIES

Adventurous Mementos

Sandy Hill's childhood in northern California imbued her with a love of mountains and inspired her to climb the highest peaks on each of the seven continents. A former cable television executive and a contributing editor at *Vogue,* Hill has become an avid spokesperson for the outdoor life and is arguably the country's most notable mountain climber. "And yet," she stresses, "climbing expedition-style is a more meditative activity than the world would think. It's really a walking meditation, both slow and deliberate."

Hill's country home in the rolling hills of northern Connecticut is where she escapes on weekends to unwind after her busy weekdays in New York as a magazine writer, book author (*Summits of My Soul*), and fund-raiser for such organizations as the New York City Ballet, the Robin Hood Foundation, and the Gay Men's Health Crisis. Both in the city and in the country, a rigorous exercise program is part of Hill's daily regimen; to prepare for the rigors of a climb, she intensifies her program of rope climbing, leg curls, triceps pushdowns,

ABOVE: Sandy Hill in her private sanctuary.
BELOW: The entrance to the Tibetan tent under brilliant Connecticut autumn sunshine.
OPPOSITE: A detail of the handwork on the tent.

stair climbing, and running.

"All of us need some sort of private space," she says, and for her this is a rainbow-colored Tibetan tent purchased from local craftsmen while en route to Mount Everest. Set on the grounds of her Connecticut house, it is filled with pieces that have "emotional and spiritual value to me. Everything in this space is necessary to my well-being."

Mementos of an adventurous life are gathered here. A collapsible snowshoe chair sits by a low wooden table displaying an eclectic assortment of objects, including horns picked up on the plains of Africa, a collection of rocks, sticks, and bones (a rock commemorates each summit she has reached), and a flask filled with Jack Daniel's whiskey, which always accompanies Hill on her climbs. Her grandfather's fishing pouch from Alaska, a whalebone from the Arctic, and a Tibetan bracelet keep company with her young son's drawings and a large cup for café au lait. Against one side of the tent, on a raised plank, is a manual typewriter. "Here I'm surrounded by the things that give me inspiration to think and to write," Hill says. "These mementos are reminders of my journeys, and somehow manage to trigger my imagination."

ABOVE LEFT: Correspondence, a laptop, a miniature globe, a favorite compass, and sunflowers are some of the special treasures that fill the worktable in Hill's tent.
ABOVE RIGHT: More memorabilia: lanterns from expeditions and a collection of rocks.
RIGHT: Along one wall is a lace panel that serves as a fresh-air window in front of an impromptu desk.

A Peaceful Palette

Charlotte Moss is a well-known New York decorator, retailer, author of several design books, and the creator of a line of furniture inspired by celebrated women of the early twentieth century such as Coco Chanel and Elsie De Wolfe. In addition to her professional life, she and her husband maintain homes in New York and East Hampton, and she somehow finds the time to work with a number of charitable organizations, including the Irvington Institute for Medical Research and Boys Harbor.

Her decision to create her own personal space was, on one level, a very practical one. "The desk in my bedroom was annoying to look at," Moss recalls. "I just can't relax and sleep with files and stacks of correspondence staring at me! So I converted one of our guest rooms into a sitting room for myself."

Moss was fortunate to have an extra guest room that she was able to transform, but her advice to women is to "find a place in your home and claim it! All of us today play a lot of roles," she notes. "We need to preserve our energy when we can, so we can focus and redirect it when necessary. My advice is to do it now. Convert a closet, use a screen to create a space within a room, anything—do it before someone else in the family

TOP: Charlotte Moss in her sitting room.
ABOVE: An embroidered silk catchall collects photographs, cards, correspondence, and invitations.
OPPOSITE: A peaceful floral Bennison fabric covers the walls and sofa, creating a soft-patterned backdrop for the small room.

stakes a claim to the space!"

The primary design strategy for Moss's sitting room was consistent with that for every other room in her apartment—"it is lined and stacked with books." Additionally, she chose a peaceful color palette of sage, ivory, and pale pink as a backdrop. "I've always admired the way the French use materials," she notes, "taking a fabric and covering the wall, the bed, and the furniture with it. It's the ease and simplicity of this approach that makes it work—the French have always understood that."

A soft floral linen from Bennison was therefore selected to cover three walls, and the fourth wall is mirrored. A soft sage green carpet lies underfoot. The large desk chair is sized just right to accommodate Moss and one of her spaniels, and a collection of sketches and watercolors of interiors covers one wall.

This room works perfectly for Moss, helping her to fulfill her many responsibilities. "This is where I bring work home from the office; I write letters for charity events; my household files are here. I write my books here. And, at the end of the day, I read and relax and listen to music!"

ABOVE: Moss's retreat, high above New York City, reflects her passion for French and English antiques and her love of books and paintings. OPPOSITE: Conveniently located adjacent to Moss's desk is a small cream-colored bookcase that houses stationery, paraphernalia, and books.

A Sculptured Space

"It just so happens I make a living doing what I love to do," says Glenna Goodacre in her pueblo-style sculpture studio in Santa Fe. Goodacre moved to New Mexico from Colorado in 1983, and in 1988 purchased the Willard Nash adobe compound, formerly the home and studio of one of the early members of the art colony established in Santa Fe in the 1920s. Leaving the original house and studio pretty much intact, she built a massive studio on the compound where she produces her much-admired sculptures, the most renowned of which is the Vietnam Women's Memorial that stands on the Mall in Washington, D.C.

"I have been a student, homemaker, wife, daughter, mother, friend, home builder, decorator, socialite, speaker, businesswoman, and cook—all while I was juggling my art career," Goodacre recalls. "Yet it was most important to me to be recognized as a 'professional artist'! Perhaps that goal was finally reached in 1994 when I was elected a member of the National Academy of Design, and when Colorado College, my alma mater, gave me an honorary doctorate."

Her bustling studio—several assistants are there most days—is spacious and airy. A skylight and numer-

ABOVE: A winding staircase leads to the balcony overlooking the studio.
OPPOSITE: The oversized fireplace mantel holds some of Glenna Goodacre's creations.

OVERLEAF: A bird's-eye view from the balcony. Wax and plaster children's heads, all studies done by Goodacre, line the top of the mirrored wall.

ous windows supply more than ample light to the room, and an oversized fireplace warms the studio.

This is Goodacre's fifth studio in Santa Fe, and with each new place, she's learned more about what she needs to facilitate creativity. "I always mirror one wall because when you reverse a piece in the mirror you can see its mistakes," she says.

"I love being here in the late afternoon, when it's just me and the answering machine. I sit in my wonderful leather chair with my feet up, reading and meditating. This is when I do those things I don't have a chance to do all day—I make lists, plan, worry, or just daydream! And the older I get, the more I value my time alone—creativity is more cerebral than active."

TOP LEFT: A weathered bench found in Mexico was installed into one wall of the new studio.
CENTER LEFT: A montage of sculpted faces by Goodacre lines the back of a door.
LEFT: The tools of her trade.
RIGHT: Goodacre in her studio.

A Grounding Room

Oprah Winfrey's busy schedule of tapings at her Harpo Productions Studio in Chicago does not allow much time for quiet relaxation. Those moments not spent in front of the camera are usually filled with meetings with her producers and staff either in her office at the studio or in what, until recently, was a rather nondescript room off her office, sometimes called "the producers' room."

"It didn't feel like it belonged to me," recalls Oprah. "The room had become a catch-all for everything, even the dogs' toys. It was a plain room, just filled with stuff! It had a couple of overstuffed chairs, some lamps I did not much care for, and paintings, boxes, awards, etc. Everybody just ignored the room."

Oprah decided to change that and asked me to work with her in creating a room that she and her staff could enjoy using. She also hoped for a place where she could find time for herself at Harpo Studios ("Sometimes I feel like I live here!") to recharge and relax, surrounded by the things she loves.

Oprah supplied me and the Chicago design firm

ABOVE: Oprah Winfrey with Sophie and Solomon.
BELOW: A triptych of dogs: from left, a pair of brass puppies; Oprah's beloved cocker spaniels; and a detail of the pastel portrait of Solomon.
OPPOSITE: Books, spirituality, and art—areas of intense and personal interest to Oprah— are evident in her room.

101

OVERLEAF: An overview of Oprah's eight-sided room with its softly glazed walls and a hand-hooked rug atop the pieced leather floor from Edelman Leathers. Favorite personal photographs and book jackets line the walls.

*OPPOSITE, CLOCKWISE
FROM BOTTOM LEFT:
A club chair finds new life
with soft leather upholstery
and a comfortable chenille
throw. A close-up of the
ever-present flower
arrangements. A script for
a possible future project.
A corner of the room
becomes a miniature gallery
displaying a favorite book
jacket matted and framed,
beneath photographs
of another special place,
Oprah's farm.*

Lovell & Associates with a "wish list," and we redesigned the room to reflect her passions—her show, her friends, her dogs, her heritage, and her love of books.

On one wall an oversized frame highlights her favorite quote, spoken by Glinda, the good witch in *The Wizard of Oz:* "You don't need to be helped any longer. You've always had the power." On another wall is a large black-and-white photograph of her award-winning staff at the Emmys. An audio-visual cabinet, formerly a dark mahogany, was lightened and stained a soft celadon shade; it holds an aubergine silk box with the script from *The Color Purple,* in which Oprah starred, along with her most recent film script, *Beloved.*

A pair of standing easels allows Oprah to spotlight and rotate cherished pieces of art. Currently featured are two of her favorite watercolor montages of her cocker spaniels, Solomon and Sophie. We reupholstered most of the existing pieces of furniture in the room, which succeeded in softening the space with lots of cozy chenille fabrics and butter-soft leathers. A rather drab wooden floor was transformed into a trompe l'oeil floor of leather, adding a soft, burnished patina underfoot.

Cove lighting was then added to the perimeter of the windowless room, resulting in a more enveloping sense of space, and walls were glazed in a soft cream strié. In total, we used four different shades of beige and off-white.

A hand-hooked rug from Elizabeth Eakins pulls together all the hues of the room and introduces a soothing new shade of blue. And to create what Oprah now calls her "grounding room," personal mementos, her Emmys, and other special awards coexist peacefully with some of her favorite books—some chosen for her book club, others because they feed her soul.

What was once a uninspired room has now become for Oprah a space for work, for celebration, and for reflection.

Enchanting Exuberance

ABOVE: *Victoria MacKenzie-Childs in her office.*
BELOW: *The inside of the cupboard, which is completely outfitted with hot and cold running water, a freezer, refrigerator, sink, and microwave.*
OPPOSITE: *A sculpture created by MacKenzie-Childs out of musical instruments flanks the side of an armoire painted with scenes of the nearby lake.*

107

Growing up as one of four children who shared bedrooms, designer Victoria MacKenzie-Childs notes that the concept of a "personal space" or a "sanctuary" would have seemed quite foreign or, at the very least, inappropriate in her family. "The topic never came up in our home," she says. "It would have been considered selfish if one of us expected some 'personal space.' When I needed to be quiet with my own thoughts and prayers I would climb a tree, take a long walk, daydream, or just tune out."

Looking back on her childhood, MacKenzie-Childs is now grateful for the discipline that it brought to her adult life. "I learned from the beginning that to be alone did not require a physical space or time," she explains. "And today, when the world is crowding in on me with activity and meetings and travel and people and pursuits, I don't need to *be* some place to find respite and peace. I have learned to find it within."

From a very young age MacKenzie-Childs was interested in art. "But every child is an artist," she says. "The question is, when does a child decide not to be an artist? I guess some people never grow up!" In her case, interest in art and design led to an enormously successful design firm. Founded by her and her artist

husband, Richard Childs, MacKenzie-Childs Ltd. is based in Aurora, a small town in upstate New York, and is known for its stylish and whimsical textiles, pottery, dishes, linens, furniture, and stationery. Today, MacKenzie-Childs Ltd. employs more than three hundred craftspeople and has retail shops and tearooms in both Manhattan and Paris.

With a demanding career and a full and active family life, MacKenzie-Child's days leave little time for solitude. But in the early morning and late at night, she does find time to be alone in her office, to catch up on correspondence and work.

With its black-and-white checkerboard walls

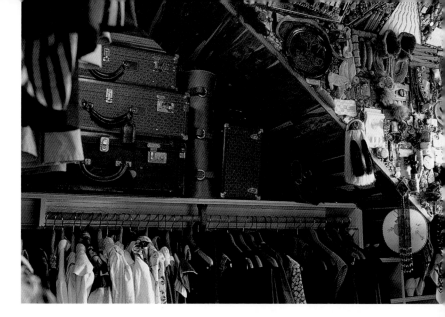

ABOVE LEFT: The Empire rattan loveseat was created at MacKenzie-Childs.
BELOW LEFT: Doorframes contrast with the checkerboard walls.
TOP RIGHT: The cedar-lined dressing room in the attic has become a collage of personal memorabilia with its three-dimensional walls.
CENTER RIGHT: An old-fashioned but reliable means of communicating in the rainbow-hued room.
BOTTOM RIGHT: Samples of MacKenzie-Childs's latest creations.

and fanciful decor, her office is an enchanting environment. One highlight is a Rube Goldberg–like rope and pulley contraption with a mushroom basket that serves to ferry notes between MacKenzie-Childs and her assistant. The office echoes the exuberant design of the MacKenzie-Childs shops and products, and it very much reflects its owner's persona.

"In a way," she observes, "I have created and decorated everything for myself. Earlier in my career I realized that whatever I did turned out more honest and purer and fresher if I did it to please me, and so everything receives a personal touch. But my real personal space," she says, "is a place in consciousness that cannot be taken from, nor added to. It is truly heaven on Earth."

A quiet sanctuary for MacKenzie-Childs is this small room with its gracious settee that opens into a bed. The "funny old lamp" and rocker came with the house, and a Swiss presser rests on an old dry goods store counter that she found in the nearby village of Aurora.

Her Personal Domain

Helen Ballard Weeks is the founder and creative force behind the Atlanta-based Ballard Designs, a successful mail-order catalog for the home and the garden. Founded in 1993, Ballard Designs has quickly established itself as one of the catalogs of choice for decorating and gardening enthusiasts of the Baby Boom generation. "I started the business because it brought together all my interests," she explains. "It includes design, photography, travel, and business. As a child I would travel with my mother and grandmother, who both collected antiques, porcelain and silver, and I think this is what nurtured my love of design."

Weeks's strenuous schedule of meetings, trade shows, and photo shoots allows her little time to spend in the space that she considers her "personal domain," namely, her office. "It's special to me," she says, "partly because I so rarely get there!" Here, surrounded by her "favorite

TOP: An olive jar holds curtain poles and finials in front of a sun-drenched window.
ABOVE: Helen Ballard Weeks at work in her office.
OPPOSITE: Weeks's "style lab" resonates with the salvage finds, ribbons, paintings, masks, fabrics, and urns that inspire her collections.

old chipped mirrors and with the art and objects my friends have made," Weeks retreats after hours or on the weekends for some well-earned quiet.

"My office is used as a 'style lab' for the business," Weeks observes. "Many of the pieces are here for product development and inspiration." The room holds architectural salvage finds, paintings, photos, magazine tearsheets, ribbons, finials, and fabrics—each one a potential source of inspiration for new ideas. "Often something is there because I am drawn to it," she says, "and then I later realize a use for it as a product in the catalog."

The contents of her "personal domain" shift and change, but the room always retains an air of relaxed comfort. "Having it appear perfect and neat is never my interest," she claims. "Instead it needs to feel like a stylish nest."

LEFT: *Against a backdrop of sheet music are pinned Weeks's favorite baby photographs.*
RIGHT: *A long view toward the bulletin board, which is a source of new ideas for Weeks.*

Because she is a voracious reader with a collection of more than three thousand books, reading and daydreaming are favorite activities here. The sheer amplitude of the room, with its oversized windows, makes Weeks feel "nice and balanced, like any space with 'good bones' can do." She utilizes bright bits of color as accents, but the palette is clearly based on the pure white of the drapes, slipcovers, and linens and on the faded colors of the old wooden objects.

A board on the wall opposite her desk changes constantly, reflecting her busy life as a creative entrepreneur. In contrast, the collection of black-and-white photographs of her children is a constant.

"Doing it all is today's biggest struggle," she says. "I've found that for me, staying in focus with the things that *really* matter is the way to stay balanced."

TOP LEFT: *A wire basket with a wooden mold.*
CENTER LEFT: *Weeks's view of her space from her curved desk.*
BOTTOM LEFT: *Softly hued ribbons offer inspiration for textures and colors.*
RIGHT: *Two mannequins create a still life.*

NINA RAMSEY

NATURAL

BECKY RUEGGER

RETREATS

AGNES BOURNE

Seaside Promontory

Founder of the design firm Archipelago and the creator of her own line of objects for the home, Manhattanite Nina Ramsey finds private sanctuary in her waterfront home on the North Fork of Long Island. "My husband, Greg, and I created this home to be a place where friends are always welcome," she explains, "so we shaped it around entertaining and people. But ironically, it's my time here alone that I find most rewarding."

Their weekend retreat is a former yacht club, complete with a large deck, that sits on a sandy spit of beach almost entirely surrounded by water. The house itself is very spare, with collections of pebbles and shells strewn across windowsills and tables, "transient mementos of the day," as Ramsey calls them. She finds her time by the sea transforming. "I undergo a kind of decompression when I am here alone," she says. "My urban life melts away and I gradually allow myself to submit to

ABOVE AND OPPOSITE: Nina Ramsey uses smooth beach stones to record favorite words.

nature's pace. I let the weather dictate my disposition: I tune in to the wind, the sea, and I begin to breathe easier."

On the faded gray wooden deck that wraps around three sides of the club, several mismatched pale green chairs surround two old white wooden tables. Nearby stands an ironing board, its angular outline evoking a slower time. Baskets of cashmere material and orange, lime, and sky blue silk fabrics—the elements of Nina's trade—line a table, forming a confetti-like tableau against the deep blue of the sea and sky.

On her seaside promontory, surrounded by the sounds and smells of the surf, Nina finds the spiritual calm that allows her to create home furnishings for others that are fresh in spirit.

TOP LEFT: *The yacht club converted to a summer home is virtually surrounded by water.*
CENTER LEFT: *Industrial-strength spools of thread.*
BOTTOM LEFT: *A hammock strung across an upstairs bedroom.*
RIGHT: *An old white table on the deck serves as an outdoor space for creativity.*

The Red Barn

ABOVE: *A long view of the barn.*
BELOW: *The accoutrements of the tack room.*
BOTTOM: *A softly worn saddle rests on bales of straw.*
OPPOSITE: *Becky Ruegger leads Josie into the barn.*

A moment of spare time is a rarity in the life of Becky Ruegger. A mother of three children, the wife of a busy corporate lawyer, the director of Gateway Project (which helps disadvantaged kids), and a catalyst in the cultural life of the New York City suburb where she and her family reside, Ruegger embraces the full life that she leads but still seeks a sense of sanctuary from her day-to-day activities.

A Vermont weekend home, reachable only by a long stretch of dirt road, is where she has carved out room to unwind and recharge. "In one sense," she observes, "the whole of our land in Vermont—the property, the mountains, streams, woods, pond, house, and barn—is my personal space. There is such reassurance in the landscape," she continues, "that all of these elements become a source of comfort."

Vermont evokes for Ruegger memories of her West Virginia childhood and a family farm in the mountains. She hopes her own children develop a reverence for nature and experience, as she did, "simplicity and freedom." Children, she feels, need a "personal space" as much as adults do: "They don't know how to nurture themselves with solitude—we need to teach them!"

It is in her barn that Ruegger finds her own private sanctuary. A classic New England red barn, it was a collaboration between Becky, her husband, Pete, and Juba

Design, a Vermont architectural firm. Together they designed a structure that was more about function than about appearance. It houses six horse stalls, a tack room, a feed room, and a spacious hayloft where Ruegger sometimes escapes to read or daydream. It is here in the early hours of the morning, alone with her two Labradors, Jordan and Magic, that she finds "moments of mindfulness and contemplation, and all the while doing the simple chores of barn keeping—mucking stalls, feeding the horses, and sweeping."

Though Ruegger shares her Vermont home with family and friends, she feels that the barn is really her own. "It gives me a connection to what I valued in my growing up," she says, "an intimate experience with nature that offers opportunity for reflection. My soul is grounded here."

LEFT: Jordon relaxing in the warmth of the Vermont sun.
ABOVE RIGHT: A mortar and pestle, used for grinding dietary supplements for the horses, catches the afternoon light.
BELOW RIGHT: Quiet time with Josie.

Campside Rejuvenation

Furniture designer and decorator Agnes Bourne's studio in San Francisco is filled with lovely photographs and paintings, but also with rocks, sticks, and feathers collected on visits over twenty-five years to her beloved ranch, the Triangle X Ranch, in Moose, Wyoming. "It's become clear to me," she says, "that my studio in San Francisco, with all its reminders of my life in Wyoming, is really just a mirror of my true 'personal space,' namely the ranch, and especially a campsite there on Mount Moran."

Bourne's life revolves around her family and her business, Agnes Bourne, Inc., which operates a showroom, design studio, and licensing company. She has designed her own line of furniture, the Agnes Bourne Collection, and has extended her business to include licensing designs for a variety of home furnishing products. In 1996, the Cooper Hewitt Museum awarded her the James Smithson Bronze Medal for her contributions to the world of design, and she is currently serving as chairman of the San Francisco Art Institute.

But as busy as her Bay Area life is, she and her family make the trip to the ranch several times a year. "It's an inspiring place," Bourne says. "In the spring and summer, flowers and baby animals and birds are every-

ABOVE: Agnes Bourne's journal against the folds of the tent wall. BELOW: The meditative atmosphere of the land inspires Bourne. OPPOSITE: The small canvas tent outlined against the backdrop of the Grand Tetons.

129

where. In the fall, herds of elk, antelope, and deer gather in the valley preparing for winter. The leaves change to gold and red and the earth seems to become very quiet."

Bourne's special place for reflection and rejuvenation is the Mount Moran campsite, almost a full day's pack trip from

*ABOVE LEFT: A makeshift table
for early-morning coffee.
ABOVE RIGHT: Bourne's pillow
is as much a sculpture as it is a
necessity on the range.
LEFT: A simple washbasin.
OPPOSITE: A red cowboy
hat and boots lie on layers of
bedding inside a tent.*

the ranch. The campsite,
which she and her family
visit year after year, has
been altered over time: logs
have been carved out to
create seats, and "foot-
stools" and "coffee tables"
have been built out of
trees to make life a bit
more comfortable. "It is not
the Ritz," notes Bourne,
"but it's the best camp
around and the scenery
simply can't be beat."

On visits to the camp-
site, she brings along only
enough to be comfortable:
riding and rain gear, sleeping bag, blankets, lanterns,
a couple of books, and, of
course, saddlebags for car-
rying back to her studio
rocks, driftwood, and other
precious artifacts.

Yet Bourne's "personal
space" is more a state of
mind than a physical site
that she can visit. It is ever
present, with the memo-
rabilia of the wilderness
serving as a constant re-
minder. As Bourne notes,
"It is the memory of being
there that gives me a feeling of peace anywhere and
allows the clearing of my
mind for new ideas."

SERENE

SPACES

GRACE MIRABELLA

ALTA TINGLE

DIANNE PILGRIM

FRANCES BOWES

ADRIENNE VITTADINI

SUSAN TORTORICI

Country Views

As editor-in-chief of *Vogue* from 1971 to 1987, Grace Mirabella presided over the greatest growth period in the magazine's sparkling history, redefining its relevance in an era when American culture, mores, and fashion were changing dramatically. After her seventeen-year stint as head of *Vogue,* she joined forces with media legend Rupert Murdoch to launch the award-winning *Mirabella* magazine; she is also a frequent lecturer on women's issues and health and recently wrote a memoir, *In and Out of Vogue.*

On weekends, Mirabella and her husband, Dr. William Cahan, leave Manhattan for their northern Westchester County home, about an hour's drive from the city. There they read, entertain, and relax in a restrained Palladian-style house designed by architect Alexander Gorlin. But much of Mirabella's time is spent in the sun-filled octagonal living room, which offers three spacious windows with unspoiled views of the countryside. In a house where no room is, as she explains, "typecast," this is where she "reads, writes,

ABOVE: Grace Mirabella in her weekend retreat with her pal, Ace.
BELOW: One of her many needlepoint pillows.
OPPOSITE: The sun-dappled octagonal room evokes a calm sensibility.

sleeps, creates, listens to music, and eats!"

In its design, the room expresses the serenity of the hills that rise beyond the windows. A comfortable white sofa is squared off on either end by a white leather chair, draped with a faux-zebra throw, and complemented by a white damask club chair

ABOVE: A close-up of the cherry wood daybed.
RIGHT: A selection of Mirabella's many books, including her own autobiography.
OPPOSITE: The living room, as seen from the dining room. Light and views of the countryside flood the room.

that holds one of Mirabella's many needlepoint pillows. A glass and chrome coffee table is usually overflowing with books and newspapers.

In the center of the room, a late-nineteenth-century sleigh bed made of rosewood and ornamented with brass ormolu is laden with her special shawls, throws from Emanuel Ungaro's couture collection in the seventies, and more of her signature pillows stitched with such bons mots as "Take time to smell the flowers" and "You're never too rich, too thin, or have too many silk blouses."

Outside, the seasons of the Northeast—lush green in the spring and summer, gold in the autumn, white and often turbulent in the winter—provide a constantly changing tableau. "Everybody needs a space where they can recharge," says Mirabella. "Where better to do this than in a room with a view?"

Manhattan Sanctuary

Museum curator Dianne Pilgrim's personal space is her apartment high above New York's Central Park West and, in particular, the corner of her living room that encompasses a wraparound terrace with a breathtaking view of the celebrated park Frederick Law Olmsted designed in 1858. Here, against this stunning backdrop, Pilgrim has assembled a first-rate collection of objects reflecting her interest in the decorative arts and design.

ABOVE: Dianne Pilgrim's love of design is nurtured by this view from her terrace window. BELOW AND OPPOSITE: Pilgrim in her Manhattan home.

139

It's an appropriate setting for the director of New York's Cooper Hewitt Museum, the Smithsonian's National Design Museum. "Design is part of everything you interact with," Pilgrim says, "whether it's a drinking cup or the Manhattan Bridge." After working on a 1973 Metropolitan Museum of Art exhibition and catalog, she went on to make her name at the Brooklyn Museum, where she was decorative arts curator for fifteen years. Ever since the fall of 1988, she has been at the helm of the Cooper Hewitt Museum, and just recently orchestrated its twenty-million-dollar renovation.

Her passion for the arts is complemented by her gritty determination to overcome obstacles. Pilgrim has multiple sclerosis and is confined to a wheelchair, but in no way has this inhibited her commitment to the Cooper Hewitt or her enthusiasm for collecting

the best of nineteenth-century American design. "Collecting," she pronounces, "always makes shopping an adventure."

Proof of these adventures, her light-filled aerie is a showcase for an eclectic array of tiles and deco objects, as well as an intriguing mélange of chairs. When she began her personal collection in the 1960s, Pilgrim decided to focus on American design from the 1830s up to the 1940s because, she notes, "no one knew about this area and it was what I could afford on a curator's salary." Her particular interest in chairs led her to assemble a wide range of styles. "Despite their variety, from a bentwood classic to some Paul Frankl rattan pieces to American Gothic dining chairs," she says, "they really work together."

ABOVE LEFT: Looking toward Central Park from the apartment balcony.
BELOW LEFT: A gleaming array of Pilgrim's choice finds.
RIGHT: The modern lines of the cabinet create a perfect stage for her pottery collection.

pots and plant containers and it is here that Pilgrim celebrates the arrival of spring each year with a party for her close friends. "I provide the plants and libations, and they do all the dirty work for me!

"During the spring, summer, and fall," she continues, "I escape to my terrace to water and weed the garden. It's my way of winding down, leaving the office behind, or else thinking about work without interruption."

Whether on the terrace or in her living-room-cum-sanctuary adjoining it, Pilgrim spends her moments of spare time entertaining good friends, reading alone, or just enjoying her unique view of downtown. "It's truly wonderful," she observes, with obvious satisfaction, "to watch darkness fall on the skyline of New York."

With Todd Black, an interior decorator and friend, Pilgrim worked to achieve a "deco" feel in the apartment. "The space is very bright and I think it really feels like a garden apartment," Pilgrim observes. "We wanted to emphasize the indoor/outdoor quality of the space and the accessibility of the terrace."

The living room furniture is art deco bamboo on a sisal carpet, with a great coffee table. On one wall is a vintage poster of the 1939 World's Fair, which is appropriate since the apartment building was built in that year.

Her slate-floored terrace holds an abundance of

TOP: The airiness of the rattan chairs complements the open feeling of the apartment.
LEFT: Two of Pilgrim's favorite chairs.
OPPOSITE: The gentle interplay of Manhattan's skyline with the terrace makes it an irresistible space.

Classical Retreat

"This nook is my own area where I am at peace, and mornings are my favorite time here. I find that the combination of nature and tranquillity inspires me creatively," says fashion designer Adrienne Vittadini, reflecting on the small pool house at her Long Island country house.

A highly successful creator of fashions for women and for the home, Vittadini works long and rewarding hours directing the far-flung operations of her international company, which, in addition to a women's fashion line and retail stores, produces a bedding collection for Cannon and a fragrance called, simply and appropriately, AV. But on weekends she and her husband, Gigi, leave their hectic New York life for their waterfront weekend home on the eastern end of Long Island.

Here, a small pool house was designed by Vittadini and architect Alexander Gorlin with columns and pillars to resemble a miniature classical temple. This is her personal refuge, a space where she can relax, recharge, and occasionally find inspiration for design ideas for her fashion collections. "I love to work out, chat on the phone, write notes to friends, and read in the pool house," says Vittadini. "The main house is usually overflowing with house guests. Here I can be alone and have some quiet time. It's also a special place for me to create because I can spread everything out on the floor in front of me."

ABOVE: Adrienne Vittadini relaxing in the shade.
OPPOSITE: Clean cotton canvas curtains, hung to let in the sea breezes when not closed for privacy, frame the view from the pool house.

ABOVE: The classical lines of the pool house are in stark relief against the deep green backdrop of the Long Island woods.
OPPOSITE, ABOVE: A collection of stylish straw hats.
OPPOSITE, BELOW: The porthole window is appropriate for the seaside setting.

OVERLEAF, LEFT: Suggestions of a summer day: goggles, sunflowers, and an inner tube.
RIGHT: Vittadini, with her hallmark crisp blue and white hues.

Located a good distance from the main house and nestled next to a pine forest, the pool house overlooks the Atlantic. It satisfies Vittadini's dual requirements for her personal space: aesthetics and convenience. "I adore the water and beautiful sun-kissed spaces, but at the same time I need accessibility to modern conveniences because I am always doing three things at once," she explains.

"And as my work as a designer evolves so does my personal space."

Filled with sunflowers, the ambience is summery, barefoot, and informal—a bit more free-spirited than the larger house. A rainy summer morning is a favorite time for Vittadini to retreat to the pool house. "With classical music—by Vivaldi, Bellini, and Schubert—this becomes my little hide-away," she says, "my little place where I am at peace."

Rustic Restraint

A mecca for garden aficionados everywhere, the Berkeley-based store The Gardener has served as a prototype for the flourishing garden shops that have accompanied the gardening enthusiasm so evident this past decade. Alta Tingle founded The Gardener in 1984, after spending much of her adult life gardening and teaching landscape design.

The shop reflects its owner's passion for and devotion to special objects for the garden and the home, from an English Sheffield pride hand shovel to hand-carved Indonesian chairs to hard-to-find goatskin gloves and one-of-a-kind sun hats. And for frustrated gardeners temporarily exiled to an apartment, Tingle's carefully edited stock of beeswax candles, topiaries, or twig and bark paper-shaded lamps can bring the aura of the garden into their lives and homes.

In her Berkeley Hills home not far from her shop, Tingle finds sanctuary from her rewarding but at times draining six-day work weeks at The Gardener. Here, in a rustic brown-shingled

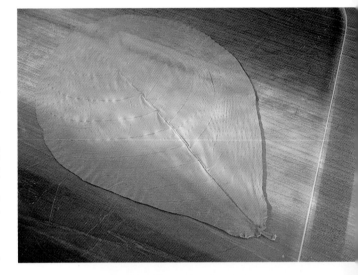

TOP: *A leaf under glass.*
ABOVE: *The unaffected simplicity of some of Alta Tingle's favorite things.*
OPPOSITE: *Tingle in a reflective moment.*

house (designed in the sixties by noted architect Felix Rosenthal) high up on the hillside, each room opens to the scent of flowers and the sight of tall sequoia redwood and eucalyptus trees.

It is here that Tingle surrounds herself with the lovely objects that mean so much to her, blurring the lines between the indoors and the outdoors. And in keeping with the spirit of the architecture, she has pared the interior of her Arts and Crafts–styled home to the basics, with a few pieces of strong furniture and walls covered with paintings by friends.

153

Her bedroom and the sleeping porch on the second floor capture the feel of living in the treetops of a magical forest, since the rooms basically serve as a wooden frame for a tranquil view. "The beginning and end of the day are my times to reflect here, to

LEFT: *The five-sided window connects Tingle to the treetops surrounding her Berkeley Hills home.*

daydream and allow ideas to formulate," Tingle says. "After being still with my thoughts, my mind then begins to hatch ideas, something like a popcorn maker. It's both a quiet and playful time that I enjoy here—maybe it's the close association with the unconscious."

Whatever this process is, it takes place in the bedroom that Tingle has come to regard as a neutral space, in complete contrast to the rest of her daily life. "All day long I seem to answer questions," she remarks. "My bedroom is my sanctuary, and although spare, it is comforting and undemanding."

The walls are lined with John Cage works on paper, and the sounds of Mozart (whom she considers an old friend) fill the air. A thick slab of glass—actually a window from a DC-3 plane—in a soft shade of turquoise rests on the writing desk, allowing an ever-changing tableau to take form underneath of pressed flowers, ferns, foliage, and cherished me-

mentos from daily life.

A chest from the Philippines resides comfortably next to a Frank Gehry chair; a Japanese cane screen does double duty as a disguise for the laundry chute behind it and as a display for new textile pieces and the shawls that Tingle wraps herself in.

Four Plexiglas cubes line one wall to keep reading matter under control, and books are piled neatly throughout the room. "I like cleanness," Tingle admits. "I feel very peaceful when I come here; things change in only small ways. I love reading in this room, especially when I can look up from my reading and see a large expanse of sky," she says.

In her bedroom, Tingle cultivates a peaceful spirit. "This room lets me take in the beauty outdoors without asking anything in return. It's as close as I get—on working days— to serenity."

155

LEFT: Plexiglas cubes bring order to Tingle's books and periodicals. The sleeping porch is to the right.

A Quiet Place

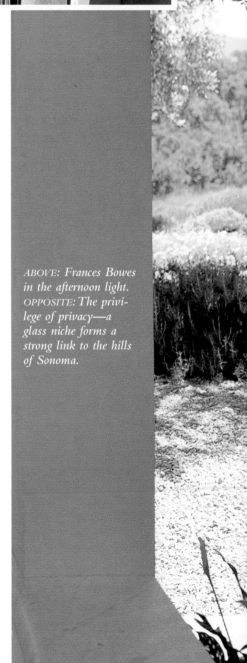

"My bathroom in Sonoma is the one quiet place I call my own," muses Frances Bowes. "It is where I can shut the door on the outside world." She and her husband, John, spend most weekends in their Sonoma Valley home, their refuge from busy weekday lives at the social and cultural center of San Francisco.

Bowes, the mother of three daughters, ran her own public relations firm for years and is now very active in the art world. She is a member of the international councils of London's Tate Museum and New York's Museum of Modern Art, vice-chair of the DIA Center for the Arts in New York, and a member of the board of the San Francisco Museum of Modern Art—all high-profile responsibilities.

But Bowes's fifteen-foot-square bathroom suggests a purity that is almost monastic in spirit. Pared down to a large porcelain tub fitted into a niche on one wall and flanked on both sides by glass doors that lead to the garden and hillside beyond, the room does not have the feel of a bathroom. And possibly because of that, or because of the freestanding furniture or the abundance of fresh flowers always present, the room embodies for Bowes the spirit of renewal. "I get a wonderful feeling of calm here," she says, "especially in the evenings.

"This spacious tub," Bowes continues, "is really a

ABOVE: Frances Bowes in the afternoon light. OPPOSITE: The privilege of privacy—a glass niche forms a strong link to the hills of Sonoma.

magnet for me. I am always cold and the warmth of the tub is very comforting. I add nice oils to the water and I always have a large bowl of good soaps and plenty of fresh washcloths within easy reach. We have music piped into our bathroom and I'll usually bring a magazine or book to read in the tub."

On the hand-rubbed plaster wall of her bathroom hangs a simple color photograph of a rose by Thomas Struth, over a small bench by John Dickerson. Standing opposite the tub is a white marble-topped dressing table, mirrored in front, on which sits a cozy grouping of family pictures and big mercury glass bowls filled with Bowes's favorite oversized bracelets and necklaces. In addition, a small square window, inspired by the Alhambra, was carefully situated to allow Bowes a view of the vineyard hills of Sonoma while bathing. The window's view is reflected in the mirror front of her dressing table.

"It's a very peaceful room," Bowes observes, "with no strong colors. I like to place wonderful-smelling flowers from the garden—freesia and daphne in winter and paperwhites and roses in summer—in big baskets and glass containers. And I always move things around," she says, "sometimes adding, sometimes putting things away in drawers just for a change."

The slower pace of the country affords Bowes a serenity not found in San Francisco. "The light is different here," she says. "We put dimmers in this room to change the mood. In the winter it's warm and comfortable. In the summer, with the doors open, a cool breeze comes in. This space is very much like Sonoma—it's calm."

TOP LEFT: A custom-designed circular mirror defines the dressing table. TOP RIGHT: Mercury glass containers hold Bowes's trademark jewelry. ABOVE: Another comfortable corner, with an inviting chaise. OPPOSITE: A collaboration with architect Ricardo Legorreta resulted in this spare yet elegant space.

Private Moments

Susan Tortorici's busy life doesn't accommodate much time for rest and relaxation. An involved participant in local cultural and social affairs, the mother of three young children who are engaged in a nonstop schedule of school and sporting activities, and the wife of an equally active television executive, her calendar is, quite simply, full. "So often I feel like I'm moving in a million directions," she notes, "trying to meet the needs and demands of so many different people in my life. I love it . . . but sometimes I feel the need to escape from it all."

TOP: *Deep drawers house personal items for quiet time. ABOVE AND OPPOSITE: A small guest room doubles as a personal space for Susan Tortorici.*

When she and Deborah Parsons of the design firm TerraCotta drew up preliminary plans for the Tortoricis' home in Pacific Palisades just outside of Los Angeles, Tortorici decided that she needed a "proper" guest room—with four walls and a separate entry—but didn't want to give up precious space to have one. The idea that emerged was to create an extension of the living room that could be closed off by pocket doors, creating a salon/guest suite. Two handsome armoires in the salon area are used as closets by guests, and the separate guest room—reminiscent of a first-class cabin on an ocean liner—has two daybeds built against its walls.

It is here in this small room, with its pillow-laden

sleeping nook, surrounded by her favorite books and photographs of her children, that Tortorici has carved her own comfort zone, where she "naps, reads, pages through catalogs, writes letters, and organizes the upcoming days. I also like to practice my flute here, privately."

In a large home filled with a busy family using every bit of available space for a myriad of activities, Tortorici has ingeniously laid claim to her own personal area where she can find the time and space to renew her energy. "On Saturday afternoons," she recounts, "I sometimes sneak in for a nap. I can't hear the phone ring, even though the room is next to my husband's office, because I put heavy-duty insulation in the interior walls. The room makes me feel like I'm on vacation in my own home!"

162

The salon, off of the living room, leads to the guest room. The oversized cherry wood armoire— one of a pair—provides visual continuity between the rooms.

EVOKING
MEMORIES

ANNA STRASBERG

DEBORAH JOHNSON

FAITH POPCORN

MARTHA BAKER

TATIANA RIABOUCHINSKA

MAYA ANGELOU

Theatrical Portraits

"This room is where I'm most private," observes Anna Strasberg. "You know, that's odd because actors have to be private in public." But the living room of her large and comfortable apartment overlooking New York's Central Park, is where Strasberg, an actress and the widow of the legendary Lee Strasberg, founder of New York's Actors Studio, finds time for her own privacy amid her breathtaking collection of memorabilia that celebrates eighty years of the American theater.

"I came into this apartment many years ago, as a young bride," Strasberg recalls. She had come to New York from her native Venezuela to work in the cultural department of the United Nations. She then entered the theater and met Lee Strasberg at the Actors Studio in 1967. They were married two years later and worked closely together until his death in 1982. Today she continues the work of her late husband at the Lee Strasberg Theater Institutes in New York and Los Angeles, is an adjunct professor at Connecticut College, and lectures and gives master classes

ABOVE: Anna Strasberg in her home.
OPPOSITE: A library ladder becomes a museum to theater greatness. A black-and-white photo of Lee Strasberg is on the lower rung.

throughout the world.

At the entrance to her living room is a large white piano once owned by Marilyn Monroe, who was a close friend and confidante of the Strasbergs. Overflowing with candles

and with framed photographs and caricatures, "it reminds me of happy times with Marilyn," Strasberg says. Windows draped with antique white linen and lace cast light on bookcases filled with more theatrical and family photographs, framed *Playbill*s, and a silver tray commemorating the first Actors Studio Award.

In front of one bookcase, a black mother-of-pearl inlaid table, covered in lace, is crowded with

even more theatrical memorabilia and objects. "This room is very important to our friends and family," says Strasberg. "It is a portrait of Lee's mind. I would change it in a minute if it ever became maudlin, but its aliveness makes it special for all who come here."

Her collection of old linens and laces covers the room's comfortable sofas, chairs, tables, and benches. "I never set out to collect them," she notes. "These

linens are a sensual thing—a continuation of my childhood. My mother had a trunkful for each of her children and she taught me to love them."

The early morning is Strasberg's time to be alone in this room. "That's when it's all mine, a word I don't use very often, and it's empty except for me. It's my time and my space in a magical place."

In the morning quiet, she reads the paper, has her breakfast, and says her prayers—"nothing intrudes on that, it's food for my soul," she emphasizes. "I have so many memories in this room, and from the window I can look down on Central Park, where I took my children when they were younger. But then at nine the phone starts ringing and the world enters." Yet she is ready for whatever the day may hold. "By then I'm centered . . . my time alone here makes me brave, gives me clarity."

Wonderfully starched laces and linens from her native Venezuela cover tables and sofas in the room.

170

African Inspirations

Deborah Johnson's days are filled with the vibrant art, fabrics, and artifacts of Africa at the Afro-American Historical and Cultural Museum in Philadelphia, where she is a buyer of objects and artifacts. At her home, not far from the museum, she has filled her living room with objects that celebrate both Africa and the female. "I decorate my space with objects that speak to me," she says, "such as candles, lots of statues, spiritual images like altar pieces, ritual masks, textiles, plants, and incense. And the statues speak to the role of female energy in African society, as figures of good luck and fertility and the bearers of spirit and children."

*ABOVE: African altar pieces and candles create a corner for meditation and reflection.
BELOW: Deborah Johnson at home.
OPPOSITE: An African mask, one of many in her collection, dominates one wall.*

This space celebrates the glory of Johnson's African heritage. A mask from the Kuba tribe in Zaire stands on an antique lampstand with pictures on the wall by the African-American artists John Biggers and Charles Searles. A windowsill is a stage for three Akuba (fertility) dolls, and a deep mud-brown oak table holds a wooden lizard box from Ghana as well as a tall, thin statue created by the West African Senufu tribe and a fish

plate from the Museum of African Art. The floor is covered with a fish rug and mud cloth from Mali, and in a corner sits the sofa, hand-painted with Adrinka symbols for peace, blessings, love, and faith. "All these things are sources of inspiration to me," Johnson explains, "and allow me to create. Everything in the room has a purpose, and all the images generate a wonderful energy for me."

Johnson points out that her living room sanctuary is notably different than the rest of the house. She observes, "It is really a spiritual place for me." This is where she meditates with candles and incense. "I read and work often here," she says. "I create in this space and often pray in it. I dance and sing here and I try to listen to myself . . . quietly."

TOP LEFT: *Assorted pillows with cowrie shells and bogolanfini (mud cloth) from Mali.*
CENTER LEFT: *African pillows and mud cloth offer contrast to the cream-colored sofa, which sits beneath Johnson's collection of masks.*
BOTTOM LEFT: *A fish plate from the Museum of African Art.*
RIGHT: *Everything in this room was chosen by Johnson for its energy and its color.*

Cottage Cocooning

"I am usually on the car phone for the entire two-and-a-half-hour trip out here. Business . . . the whole time! But that's sort of a transition period. I don't get a lot of business calls here, even though my clients all have the number. Yet no one ever calls me out here, which is so sweet." This is futurist Faith Popcorn, chairman of BrainReserve, author of the best-selling books, *The Popcorn Report* and *Clicking,* and well-known trend forecaster for corporate America, talking about her home on the eastern end of Long Island, several hours from her company's base in New York City.

Popcorn introduced the concept of "cocooning" to marketers. Fittingly, her country home is a small rose-covered cottage hidden in the woods at the end of a dirt road lined with tall evergreen trees. Behind the house is a gentle pond separated from the Atlantic Ocean by weather-beaten sand dunes and sea grass. "I originally had a bigger house out here, but I decided to move into a much smaller place," Popcorn explains. Her little cottage dates back to the late seventeenth century and was once a cookhouse; it was gradually added to over the years.

ABOVE: Faith Popcorn in front of her seaside cottage.
BELOW: A brick walk, an American flag, and a picket fence greet visitors.
OPPOSITE: Weathered Adirondack chairs are perfect companions for a warm summer afternoon.

OVERLEAF: Opposite the television cabinet is an old stone fireplace with its horseshoe screen and gilt-framed dog portraits.

ABOVE: *Photographs of family and friends flank a chaise.*
BELOW: *Overlooking the pond.*
OPPOSITE: *A painted green country-style cupboard houses Popcorn's favorite form of relaxation.*

It is here the "Nostradamus of Marketing" (as *Fortune* magazine dubbed her) sheds her city armor and settles in for a weekend of reading, meditating, taking walks, doing yoga, and playing with her dog.

"I come out here every weekend, winter, summer, spring, and fall. I'm trying to make my weekends longer, so I meditate every morning, I listen to music, and I also watch a lot of television," she says. "I adore television, and I love to watch the talk shows to see what people are thinking about."

Jimmy Topping, a good friend of Popcorn's, helped her paint the living room green. A small table holds photographs of friends and travels, and the walls and the mantel over the stone fireplace are lined with antique paintings and watercolors of favorite dogs, including Japanese pugs, Boston terriers, boxers, and an assortment of puppies.

Her television set is sequestered in a lime green armoire, along with her extensive collection of movies and CDs. And a chaise in the corner of the living room—a birthday gift from friends—is Popcorn's favorite space. "To me the combination of a book, my chaise, and my dog is perfection," she says with a smile.

window faces the back-yard with its weathered flagpole and frequently displayed American flag. "There are no curtains," Baker says, "because I like to let in as much light as possible. It's a wonderfully open and airy space."

Baker and her husband, fashion photographer Chuck Baker, foraged for the numerous antique frames that create a sort of three-dimensional wallpaper behind their massive mahogany four-poster bed. "And the room is really about this huge bed," she says. Carved in colonial Caribbean style, "it sits up high," she explains, "like a tree house, situ-ated so you can sit in bed and feel like you could dive right into the sea."

This is where Martha can be found in the early morning, with the first sunlight streaming in, planning her day or just savoring some quiet time. Throughout the rest of the house, riding boots, tennis rackets, golf clubs, life jackets, and running shoes are strewn about—remnants of an active family life. In here, however, are lovely photographs of her four children, framed in shades of sepia, cream, black, white, and gray, each one captured by her husband.

These mementos change only, Baker says, when "Chuck has taken a heavenly new shot of one of the children or a new puppy." Surrounded by the myriad objects that characterize her busy life, Martha notes with amusement, "My time-outs aren't scheduled in—I just sneak up here and hide. It's a place where I feel I can pull together my thoughts, have a private phone conversation, or just pause in my day."

ABOVE: A late-afternoon sun floods Baker's bedroom.
RIGHT: Two classics—a vintage telephone and Ralph Lauren sheets.

Reflections of the Dance

In 1932 Colonel Wassily de Basil and Rene Blum founded the Ballets Russes de Monte Carlo. The new company filled the void left by the breakup of Sergei Diaghilev's Ballets Russes in 1929 and quickly established itself as a major force in the ballet world until its dissolution in 1948. One of the company's brightest stars—and one of its three internationally acclaimed "baby ballerinas"—was the legendary Tatiana Riabouchinska. She was a prima ballerina during that exciting and glamorous era, a memorable epoch when the Ballets Russes attracted and developed some of the finest dancers and choreographers of the century.

After leading, as she says, "a very exotic life," Riabouchinska, known as Tanya, settled in Los Angeles. There she and her husband, David Lichine—a dancer, librettist, and choreographer with the company—opened a ballet school in Beverly Hills and directed several groups, including the first Los Angeles Ballet. Today, at the age of eighty-one, she lives in Mandeville Canyon, California, where she still conducts two dance classes a day at her studio.

Riabouchinska's special retreat is the living room of her home and, in particular, the area around her red

ABOVE: Tatiana Riabouchinska in her California home.
OPPOSITE: A few treasured programs from Ballets Russes performances around the world.

brick fireplace, which is lined and stacked with memories of her career as a dancer and choreographer—photographs, programs, albums, and books abound. "After my classes, I'm naturally very tired, and so this is a restful place to be," she explains.

Here she has created, with the help of her good friend Lynn von Kersting, an intimate corner that offers images of a fulfilled life and the restorative tonic of solitude. Her retreat resonates with the vivacity that she brought to the stages of Paris, London, Brazil, Australia—"I danced everywhere," she recalls.

A weathered wicker sofa is covered in mattress ticking and made comfortable with old floral cushions and plump pillows. An oversized ottoman with its original green paint and floral remnants sits in front of the sofa; atop it rests an antique tea tray and a sketchbook autographed by her fellow dancers in the Ballets Russes. Overblown old-fashioned roses throughout the room accentuate the nostalgic and romantic mood of her place, as the soft summer light of southern California filters through the lace-draped window. It's a peaceful sanctuary, rightly celebrating a long, rewarding, and adventurous life.

The chains and slavery's coffles
The whip and lash and stock.

My fathers speak in voices
they shred my fact and sound
They say "It's our submission
that makes the world go round."

They used the finest cunning
their naked wits and wiles
the Lowly Uncle Tomming
and Aunt Jemima's smiles

They've laughed to shield their crying
Then shuffled through their dreams
And stepped'n fetched a country
To write the blues with screams

I understand their meaning
it could and did derive
from living on the edge of death
They kept my race alive.

Gather Together In My Name
..."Baby, Mother Dear's going to tell
you something about life."...
..."People will take advantage of
you if you let them. Especially
Negro women. Everybody, his brother and his dog, thinks he can
walk a road in a colored woman's
behind. But you remember this,
now. Your mother raised you.
You're full-grown. Let them
catch it like they find it. If
you haven't been trained at home
to their liking tell them to get
to stepping.'... 'Stepping. But
not on you.
"You hear me?"
"Yes, Mother. I hear you."

The Heart Of A Woman
..."Sit down baby. I'm going to
tell you something you must
never forget."
..."Never, never let a person know
you're frightened. And a group of
them...absolutely never. 'Fear'
brings out the worst thing in
everybody. Now, in that lobby you
were as scared as a rabbit. I
knew it... If I hadn't been there,
they might have turned into a
mob. But something about me told
them, if they mess with either of
us they'd better start looking for
some new asses. 'cause I'd blow
away what their mammas give
them."
She laughed like a young girl.
"Look in my purse." I opened her
purse.
"The Desert Hotel better be ready
for integration. 'Cause if it's not,
I'm ready for the Desert Hotel."

..."Take care of yourself. Take
care of your son, remember...
Black folks can't change because
white folks won't change. Ask
for what you want and be pre-
pared to pay for what you get."

I Know Why The Caged Bird
Sings
..."During the picking season my
grandmother would get out of bed
at four o'clock (she never used an
alarm clock) and creak down to her
knees and chant in a sleep-filled
voice, 'Our Father, thank you for
letting me see this New Day. Thank
You that you didn't allow the bed I
lay on... to be my cooling board, nor
my blanket my winding sheet. Guide
my feet this day along the straight
and narrow, and help me to put a
bridle on my tongue. Bless this
house and everybody in it. Thank
You, in the name of your son,
Jesus Christ, Amen."
"The truth is a stubborn fact."...
                Maya Angelou

Poetic Harmony

Dr. Maya Angelou's distinguished and multifaceted career has propelled her on a fascinating journey from her birthplace in St. Louis to a myriad of cities around the world.

Her travels have ranged from Tel Aviv in the early '60s, where she taught modern dance at the Rome Opera House, to Cairo, where she was an associate editor of the English-language news weekly, *The Arab Observer,* to Ghana, where she taught at the national university, and finally, back to the United States, where she became a best-selling author (*I Know Why the Caged Bird Sings*) and playwright, an Emmy-nominated actress (for her role in *Roots*), and, of course, perhaps the country's best known poet for the presentation of her poem "On the Pulse of Morning" at President Clinton's inauguration in 1993.

Home for Dr. Angelou is Winston-Salem, North Carolina, not far from the Wake Forest University campus where she is the Reynold's Professor of American Studies. Here, in a large, rambling house, she unwinds from her vigorous schedule of speaking and writing, and replenishes body and soul for her next project. "Easy reading," she notes, "is very hard writing. I think it was Hawthorne who said that."

*ABOVE: Dr. Maya Angelou in her North Carolina garden gazebo.
BELOW: A comfortable armchair in front of the living room fireplace is where she reads and relaxes.
OPPOSITE: "Maya's Quilt of Life," commissioned by her friend Oprah Winfrey and created by Faith Ringgold, covers one living room wall.*

193

"I come out at six-thirty in the morning, plug in a pot of coffee, and basically just sit here," says Dr. Angelou. "I don't do a lot of work at home but I do find the gazebo is a wonderful place to edit what I've written. The wind blows through and clears out my brain."

In her living room hangs "Maya's Quilt of Life," a remarkable kaleidoscope of words and fabrics celebrating Dr. Angelou's life. It serves as an exuberant backdrop to her extensive collection of art by African-American artists, gathered by Dr. Angelou over the past thirty years. "I find it relaxing to search out art," she explains. "I love to sit in this room at night with a bowl of soup, surrounded by my paintings. I let them be my guide."

Different rooms in the house provide the sanctuary and relaxation that she seeks. In the kitchen, she likes to find herself "something really complex to cook. Cooking consumes my whole focus, my thinking, all my senses. I like seeing it, I like smelling it, I like touching it. The work recedes into the background."

A backyard screened-in gazebo overlooks her extraordinary garden and pool.

ABOVE: *The hand-carved mahogany chaise is covered in a ruby and cream damask; it sits under a painting by Samella Lewis.*
OPPOSITE, CLOCKWISE FROM TOP LEFT: *A carved "joy" rock in the garden; a corner of the living room; some of Dr. Angelou's countless books; a quiet morning in the gazebo; a detail of a painting.*

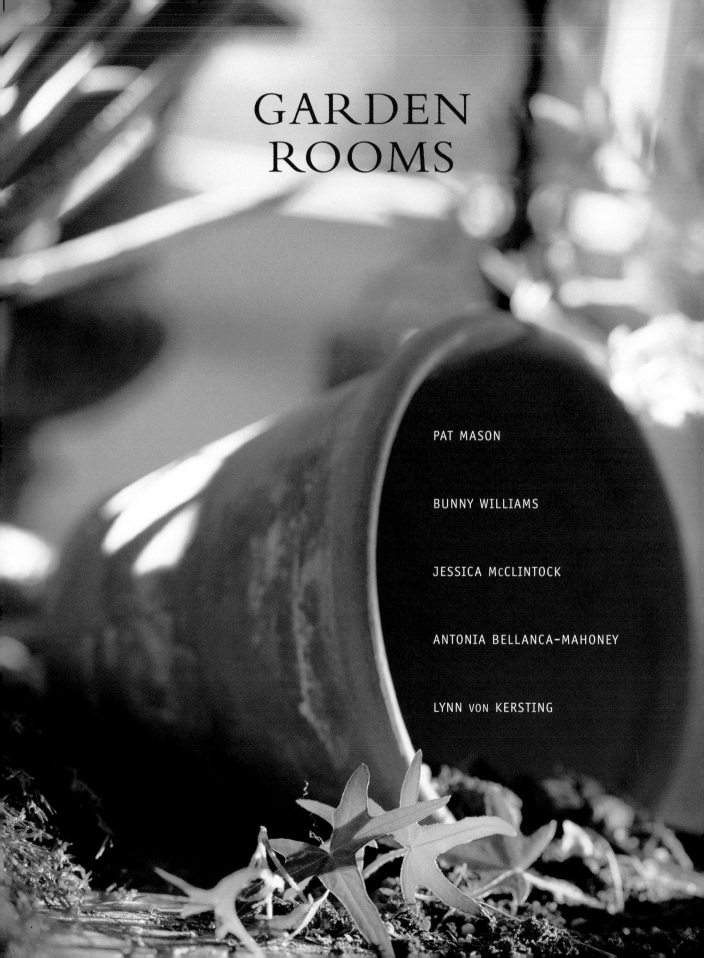

GARDEN ROOMS

PAT MASON

BUNNY WILLIAMS

JESSICA McCLINTOCK

ANTONIA BELLANCA-MAHONEY

LYNN von KERSTING

Pavilion by the Sea

From Monday to Friday for most of the year, Pat Mason is busily and happily engaged in her professional life as a realtor and vice president of the New York City real estate firm William B. May, where she has specialized for over thirty-five years in the sale of town houses in lower Manhattan. "I'm obsessive about houses and clients and trying to make the perfect fit," she says.

But on Friday evenings, she and her husband, Francis Mason, the editor of *Ballet Review* and a radio voice familiar to listeners of New York's WQXR Radio, arrive at their weekend home in a water-front community about an hour's drive from their Greenwich Village town house. Backed by a deep nature preserve and facing the waters of Long Island Sound, their charming white clapboard house is notable both for its lush English-style gardens and for its soaring white garden room. Fashioned in the shape of a pavilion—a perfect eighteen-foot-square room that reaches up twenty-four feet to a peaked skylight—it was created and built with ar-

ABOVE: Seed packets and gardening magazines are treasured fodder for the gardener.
OPPOSITE: Pat Mason in her pavilion.

ABOVE: A bust of Mason as a young child stands next to the oversized French doors that lead to the garden.
BELOW: Rossant and Mason's collaboration resulted in an airy white tower that suggests the peaked tents that dotted the battlefield at Agincourt.
OPPOSITE: A hand-carved oak birthing chair gains a second life in the garden conservatory.

chitect James Rossant several years ago.

Mason recalls her first discussion with Rossant regarding the project. "He was somewhat uninterested when I originally put the problem to him and, in fact, suggested I buy a ready-made item. But six months later, he suddenly called and said he had a good idea."

Challenged by the Masons' vision, Rossant presented them with plans for a garden room wing that addressed Pat Mason's main requirements: a room where she could grow her semitropical plants in the winter, have cozy lunches on winter days and casual suppers on warm summer nights, and above all, just relax and read, surrounded by her beloved plants.

With its three oversized French doors and an abundance of windows, the pavilion fulfills Mason's vision. Flowers are indeed everywhere: old-fashioned abutilon, perennial blue morning glories, lush *Solandra maxima.* "Right now there's a magical purple curtain of *Verbena bonarensis* that self-sowed itself in the rocks outside the French doors," she says.

And within this unique space, she finds time for herself. "I take care of my plants, look at the garden, read garden catalogs and wonderful books on gardens. I make my wish lists for the garden. Here I can catch up on my letters and correspondence. I also find that when I'm relaxing here I have my most creative thoughts about my business. I love thinking about my deals while I'm fussing around in here."

Rossant's design suggests both a lighthouse and, he notes, the medieval peaked tents that Mason admires. With its central skylight, the room receives morning, afternoon, and late-day sun.

"I often get up early in the morning and catch a particularly wonderful sunrise, or else I have a drink at sunset," Mason says. "With the placement of the windows, the sun is perfectly framed for me. The room itself turned out to be perfect!"

A Passion for Potting

Exotic, one-of-a-kind garden ornaments from all around the world are everywhere in Treillage, a gardener's fantasy shop that belongs to Bunny Williams. It's natural, then, that her favorite place to unwind would be her potting shed in the country. "Being in this room is sheer fun . . . potting, repotting, working with my hands is relaxation for me," says Williams.

Never one to sit still, Williams not only designs for and directs Treillage, along with co-owner John Rosselli, but is also renowned in this country and abroad for her interior design acumen. Her career began at the English antiques dealer Stair and Company. She then joined the firm of Parish-Hadley, where she worked with the legendary Sister Parish and the equally legendary Albert Hadley. She founded her own design firm in 1988 and three years later opened Treillage in an old blacksmith shop on New York's East 75th Street. Since then, Treillage, with its array of gardening pieces and pleasures, has become a veritable magnet for garden lovers.

Two hours north of the city, in a part of Connecticut notable mainly for its lovely farms and abundant antiques shops, Williams sheds her city routines and takes up the country life in a two-hundred-year-old Federal-style home. Here she pursues and nourishes her passion for gardening in a weather-beaten potting

ABOVE: Bunny Williams in her potting shed.
OPPOSITE: Afternoon sun falls on the potting shed workbench, with antique watering cans, an assortment of pots, and a perfect topiary.

shed that was part of the original house.

"My rhythm is much slower here," she says. "Though it takes a lot of discipline and focus to transplant seedlings, for example, it gives me a wonderful calmness. It is actually a very humbling experience because in the end, nature has its way.

"To me this shed is perfect imperfection. I love its layers of age and that it is essentially unchanged from when the house was first built."

204 Unchanged, yes, but the room itself bears the signature of Williams's touch: lots of wonderfully aged watering cans, birds' nests, and two wheelbarrows, one filled with raffia, another with gardening stakes. Although an old lift-top school desk forms a serene still life in the center of one wall, it's also practical. Filled with catalogs and how-to books, it is where Williams sits and records in her diary what's in bloom in her many gar-

Three ruby-toned dahlias are the perfect accent pieces for Williams's "planning and dreaming garden desk."

dens. A window above looks out onto her kitchen garden, while the other window allows her to watch her dogs playing on the lawn.

"I design, dream, and plan here," Williams says. "It's an escape from a very hectic world, where I'm usually doing ten things at once. Here, whether it's stormy or sunny outside, it's a calming experience."

And the multitude of tools for her trade—potting soil, bulbs, plant nutrients, terra-cotta pots and chips, chicken wire, and seed packets—confirm the spirit of her nurturing shed. Atop a storage cabinet, a row of luminescent glass bulb-forcing jars catch the last glint of the afternoon sun, reflecting a prism of colors and all the possibilities of this serene space.

LEFT: The late-afternoon light forms a silhouette of the bulb jars onto the weatherbeaten cabinet.
RIGHT, CLOCKWISE FROM TOP LEFT: A miniature wooden wheel barrel and a bee keep basket; bamboo sticks and a watering can; a painted wicker rocker at the entrance to the shed among the tools of a busy gardener; the old door reflecting a late fall afternoon; terra-cotta shards to be used for lining pots.

Garden Lace

Designer Jessica McClintock's favorite quotation—"It is only with the heart that one can see rightly; what is essential is invisible to the eye"—is from *The Little Prince*. "I've always felt that," she explains. "It was like a nod in my heart when I read it." And following her heart has proven to be an exceptionally judicious business philosophy for McClintock.

Launching her business career with her company Gunne Sax, which flourished during the "flower child" days of the '70s, she went on to found Jessica McClintock Inc. to encompass a wide range of social, bridal, junior, and children's dresses. In addition to her wholesale business, McClintock has opened twenty-three boutiques around the country and has also created two best-selling fragrances, Jessica McClintock and Jess.

McClintock's home in San Francisco is a mirror of her fashion philosophy—gracious, soft, and feminine. Although it offers a sense of sanctuary throughout, there is for McClintock one space, in particular, that evokes relaxation and renewal. Looking out onto a small French courtyard is a garden room, perfectly symmetrical with enormous arched windows at one end and a small demilune niche. This is her private corner.

The centerpiece of the garden room is a crochet-covered table situated in the circular alcove, where

ABOVE: Jessica McClintock in her garden room.
BELOW: In a nook against the hand-rubbed plaster walls is a bust of a young French girl.
OPPOSITE: The light-filled garden room is where McClintock goes to sketch and reflect.

209

McClintock plans designs for each new season. "I love to read here and research themes for new designs," she explains. Beneath the crochet cloth is an iridescent Duppioni silk underskirt in a pale shade of desert peach, which picks up the delicate tones of the room's inlaid peach marble floor.

The objects in this garden room reflect McClintock's search for the unique and the romantic. An eighteenth-century French chair, she says, was discovered in Marin and is "my favorite chair in the house. I'm a small person and it's sized just right for sitting and sketching." A metal fruit stand, chosen for its "lovely lacy effect," was picked up at auction, as was the pickled French cabinet that stands at the far end of the room. And a television set is ingeniously hidden in the cabinet for those occasional times when she dines alone.

"Everyone needs downtime," McClintock stresses. "Mine consists of looking at romantic European movies, especially Merchant-Ivory movies, such as *A Room With a View* and *Howards End*. I love the mood in this room, because of its garden feel. And most of the time it's quiet," she says, "except for music. Listening to classical music and absorbing the beautiful view of the gardens simply inspire me."

ABOVE LEFT: Afternoon tea.
ABOVE RIGHT: A view of the French courtyard, designed by Willis Polk, with the garden room on the right.
RIGHT: The Pleyel piano, purchased from an antiques dealer in France, is the same make that Mozart practiced on.

Fragrant Hideaway

"Men have always understood the need for a special place—their hunting cabin, fishing boat, favorite car, woodworking shop, their little shack down by the pond, or even their reclining chair in the den," muses Antonia Bellanca-Mahoney as she takes a moment for herself in a small room next to her pool and garden. "Women have such constant demands between work and family that time and space to recharge is a *must* to maintain equilibrium."

Equilibrium, or the fine art of balancing it all, is practiced daily by Bellanca-Mahoney, a Long Island woman and mother of two, whose nose and intuition led her to create the best-selling fragrance, Antonia's Flowers. Inspired by the scents of her Sicilian grandmother's garden on Long Island, where she spent many hours as a child, Bellanca-Mahoney opened up her first flower shop at the young age of twenty-four, in East Hampton, Long Island. She quickly developed an outstanding reputation for her floral arrangements, which led her in 1984 to create her classic freesia-scented fragrance, today sold throughout the world.

Nestled among her beloved fields of flowers and just steps away from the Tuscany-inspired home that she and her husband, Stephen, built, is her sanctuary from it all. This is a twenty-five-foot-square room with creamy

ABOVE: Antonia Bellanca-Mahoney at ease in her pavilion.
OPPOSITE: Sunflowers from her nearby gardens front a simple iron bed accented with the sunshine and the sea colors of her linens.

white walls and a slate floor, as well as a glass-fronted garage door that allows her to keep an eye on the world. A large slab of driftwood hangs high on one wall and holds shells and other treasures. Beloved pieces have been brought to her pavilion, like an old iron daybed that Bellanca-Mahoney saved especially for this room. "I think it's everyone's fantasy to have a great big bed or chair away from it all," she says. "This room works for me—I've made it my own with shells, linens, and, of course, flowers."

She has the good fortune to work among the flowers, shrubs, and plants that she adores. She has the added good fortune of being able to rest in this small space that she has created. "I have finally discovered my most secret desire," she says with a smile. "It's a place to nap, to read a magazine, to simply drift off."

ABOVE LEFT: A pool house with a garage-style door becomes Bellanca-Mahoney's private retreat.
BELOW LEFT: A sea of clematis.
RIGHT: She surrounds herself with the glories of her garden.

Gilt-Edged Spirit

Nestled discreetly in the hills above Sunset Boulevard in Los Angeles is a Caribbean pink house once owned by the film director George Cukor. Its owner today is Lynn von Kersting, who, along with her companion, Richard Irving, has meticulously reclaimed the structural integrity of the house while retaining its wonderful spirit. This, after all, was once the gathering spot for generations of Hollywood luminaries, such as Somerset Maugham, Katharine Hepburn, Spencer Tracy, Cary Grant, and, more recently, Lily Tomlin, who recalls, "I hardly said a word there—I was so awed!"

After Cukor died in 1983, the house remained on the market for over two years. When von Kersting and Irving moved in in 1985, they realized its underpinnings were in dire need of restructuring, and so von Kersting went about the work with the zest she brings to all her projects. Her life is a full one—interior designer, owner of the chic design shop Indigo Seas, restaurant owner (The Ivy, Ivy at the Shore), and mother of a young daughter. Although glamorous and fulfilling, her work

TOP: An exterior view of the rose-covered oval room. ABOVE AND OPPOSITE: The sun-splattered sitting room, with its reminiscences of an ocean liner, reflects the romantic sensibilities of Lynn von Kersting.

can stretch from early-morning design conferences to late nights at the restaurants.

Home, and in particular an oval-shaped sitting room, is where von Kersting finds time for solitude, inspiration, and rejuvenation. "This oval room is like a stateroom on an oceangoing yacht," she rhapsodizes. "With its blue walls and shuttered windows, it's a cool retreat."

A nicely faded blue-green rug serves as a soft anchor for the gilt-edged room filled with memories and reminiscences for von Kersting. Books are piled high everywhere. There are stacks of opera librettos, Hungarian roses, and the incredible pieces that von

TOP LEFT: *A 19th-century japanned highboy with French and Moroccan lavender from her gardens, a thirties shell vase, and a collection of shells in front of a portrait of Ina Claire.*
CENTER LEFT: *Fresh mint leaves from the garden fill a lovely vase.*
BOTTOM LEFT: *White roses in a majolica dish.*
RIGHT: *On the table stands a 19th-century Baccarat candelabrum with waterfall pendants. On the wall is a collection of 19th-century American and English dog paintings.*

Kersting either inherited or discovered on her forays around the globe: a nineteenth-century Italian daybed, a bleached-wood Chinese Chippendale table, a nineteenth-century japanned highboy, and, for a touch of whimsy, a nineteenth-century bust of Shakespeare wearing a Turkish hat at a rakish angle.

A timeless space, with no sharp edges or angles, the room seems comfortable with both its stylish past and stylish present.

"It's like a mixture of old summer house memories," von Kersting says. "Everything feels at home in this curious room—it really has a lot of soul to it. It invites me to sift through my records, open a book, count my blessings. To quote our friend Mr. Truman Capote, 'Home! And happy to be.'"

The graciously curved room forms a poignant link to the past with its Italian daybed in the foreground and the romantic vignettes of von Kersting's life: an Italian gilt mirror, a miniature Kashmiri summer palace, a 1930s papier-mâché dog, and stacks of books, both rare and authored by her many friends.

index

from the sky

PHOTO CREDITS
*All of the photographs in this book are by Jennifer
     Lévy except for the following:*
Helga Ancona: page 50
Chuck Baker: pages 183 (below), 186
Lizzie Himmel: pages 8–9, 13 (above left), 16, 17,
     26–31, 66–71, 118–123, 144–148, 182, 183
     (above), 187, 212, 213, 214 (below), 215
     (top left, center left, bottom left, top right)
Lexie Shabel: pages 78–83
Christopher Simon Sykes: page 157
Marlene Wallace: page 41
Courtesy of Harpo Productions: page 101
     (top right)